Black Folk Tales
· AND CHRONICLES OF ·
South Carolina

Black Folk Tales

• AND CHRONICLES OF •

South Carolina

DAMON L. FORDHAM

THE
History
PRESS

Published by The History Press
Charleston, SC
www.historypress.com

Back cover: *The Parting Song,* by A.R. Waud, *Harper's Weekly,* November 9, 1867. *Library of Congress.*

First published 2025

Manufactured in the United States

ISBN 9781467158251

Library of Congress Control Number: 2024945298

"Decoration Day," *Harper's Weekly*, June 4, 1881, by S.G. McCutcheon. *Library of Congress*.

Contents

Preface

I collect stories as other people collect stamps.

I was of that last generation of young people who loved to listen to the elders tell stories to pass the time, share history and teach life lessons. Prior to the advent of radio and television, this was how generations of people passed their spare time. This was especially true in the southern United States and particularly of the Black population.

Every ancient culture once had its equivalent of wise and humorous tellers of tales who preserved their history and taught lessons through expressive storytelling. The Irish had the *seanchaí*; the Chinese had the *pingshu*; the English had wandering minstrels, who told the tales of King Arthur and Robin Hood; Arabs had the *hakawati*, who told tales from the likes of the Holy Koran and *The Arabian Nights*; and West Africa had the *griots* (gree-ohs). The latter were often the only sources of history in preliterate societies, and the storytellers I heard in my youth were the direct spiritual descendants of the African griots.

Folk tales and storytelling were among the means with which African Americans coped with their predicament, but their preservation has been complicated. The white Georgian Joel Chandler Harris used the tales of enslaved Black storytellers, such as "Uncle" George Terrell, for his *Uncle Remus* books of the late 1800s and early 1900s. These books popularized the genre, but the white collector of Black folklore tended to be at a disadvantage. These tales were a major part of Black American culture during the days of lynching and segregation, thus Black people were less than candid in sharing their stories with white or educated Black people whom they did not know well. This accounts for the occasionally positive views of slavery given to white interviewers. Thomas A. Talley, in his 1923 folklore collection, *The Negro Traditions*, noted, "They did not tell him all the story, because no ex-slave at that time was so foolish to run the risk of incurring the ill will of a white man by going through with a story in which one of that race was held up to ridicule."[1] Fortunately, this volume collects many stories from subjects who were interviewed by Black chroniclers, such as Augustus Ladson, Laura Middleton and the staff of the South Carolina Negro Writers' Project and the compliers of *Humorous Folk Tales of the South Carolina Negro*, which results in a more honest accounting of their experiences.

Additionally, the educated and literate Black people of that era were largely assimilated into white American culture (as much as could have been possible in the age of segregation). Many had a tendency to scorn these folk tales and this culture of storytelling as "backward," "ignorant" and "slavery time talk" that they wished to put behind themselves, as they viewed them as threats to their desires to assimilate into mainstream America. At the same time, many Black adults would not pass such stories down through the generations, as it was commonplace for them to not allow their children to listen to what they called "grown folks' talk" and send the young people away. A tragic result was that many interesting stories were lost to the graveyards, and Black folklore is largely a lost art, as it is extremely rare to find a young person who specializes in the telling and study of such folk tales.

Another problem was that white and Black authors usually wrote such tales with a thick southern dialect and a now-archaic version of "Black English" that was designed at best to replicate the speech patterns of their informants—or, at worst, to mock the "otherness" of said informants. The unfortunate effect of this technique has been to render such stories unintelligible to the modern reader. Therefore, I have modified the use of written dialect to make the stories easier to understand for the contemporary reader while retaining the richness of the tales. However, to preserve the historical integrity of the original stories, I have, in most cases, retained the use of terms found in such tales that are no longer in popular or polite use. It is hoped that the sensitive reader will understand the context of such usage. A good number of the stories were also transcribed by people who had little insight or understanding of the culture of those whom they interviewed, and it shows in some of the stories that were transcribed in an incoherent fashion. I have occasionally edited the tales from their original sources for the sake of clarity.

This is also the case with the Gullah stories in this book. The tales of the working-class Black population in the Lowcountry and Charleston area of South Carolina, who retained elements of their African speech and customs from isolation, appear. As this tonal form of speech does not translate well in its original form, I have modified it to make such stories understandable to the average reader, but a few stories, such as my grandmother's tale regarding my grandfather and his pipe, have retained elements of phonetic Gullah speech.

An editorial in Columbia's Black newspaper, the *Palmetto Leader*, on April 19, 1930, challenged Black writers: "For the person of real ability, there is much to be discovered right here in South Carolina. Think of all the white people who have gained fame by writing about South Carolina Negroes! Our situation is analogous to the man who abandoned a rich oil field because it would not bear cotton. If our naiveté must be exploited, why not exploit it ourselves?" This volume attests to the truth of that statement.

Fortunately, in my youth, my parents and other adults willingly shared a lot of oral history and folklore with me, much of which I wrote down over the years. As a child, I found such stories fascinating, and in the summer of 1977, at the age of twelve, I came across B.A. Botkin's *A Treasury of American Folklore* and Zora Neale Huston's *Mules and Men* in our neighborhood library. These books alerted me to the fact that the stories I heard from my elders were special and precious parts of our culture, which, even then, were on the verge of extinction. Over the years, I would collect the anecdotes of my elders in notebooks. These tales appear in the final chapter of this volume. During a couple of sojourns to West Africa, I collected the tales from the griots, the oral historians of that region. As a background to the South Carolina material that encompasses most of this book, I have included a chapter of these African stories.

Other chapters contain material from rarely used public domain sources, such as Abbie Holmes Christensen's *Afro-American Folk Lore* (1892), Elsie Clews Parson's *Folk Lore of the Sea Islands: South Carolina* (1923), The South Carolina Negro Writers' Project (1936–37) and J. Mason Brewer's *Humorous Folk Tales of the South Carolina Negro* (1945), as well as miscellaneous newspaper accounts. I have included such rare accounts as testimonies of intriguing anecdotes from the attempted Denmark Vesey Slave Rebellion of 1822. The final chapter contains tales and family stories that I remembered from childhood, including selections from the journal of my father, Abraham Fordham Jr., and from interviews I've conducted in recent years. Narratives and interviews from Black South Carolinians, most previously unpublished, give added dimension to our understanding of Black life in South Carolina in the same era.

It is hoped that this book will awaken people to the importance of preserving the tales of their elders. Its purpose is best summed up in the introduction of what is perhaps the world's best-known collection of folk tales, *One Thousand and One Nights*, also known as *The Arabian Nights*:

> *The tales of former generations are a lesson to the living; that a man may look back on the remarkable events which have happened to others, and may consider the history of those who came before him, gain from their wisdom, and learn from their mistakes. Extolled be the perfection of those who have learned the history of former generations to be a lesson to those which follow. Such are the stories of the Arabian Nights, with their tales of adventures and their fables.*

A Note on the References:

The names of the storytellers, where known, are listed below each story. Further notices, such as the books or other sources for the tales, appear in the endnotes. The original titles of stories are given, so sensitive readers be warned that some titles may be offensive to some contemporary standards and must be taken in the proper historical context.

Acknowledgements

Special thanks to all of the storytellers in this book, including my parents, Pearl and Abraham Fordham, and other assorted relatives and elders.

To Abby Cole of the University of South Carolina's (USC) South Caroliniana Library in Columbia, South Carolina, for the "Unpublished Ex-Slave Narratives"; Todd Hoppock of the Caroliniana Library for the photograph of Celia Dial Saxon and Black students at USC during Reconstruction; and the Caroliniana Library for its online archive of the South Carolina Negro Writers' Project.

To Georgette Mayo of the Avery Research Center in Charleston, South Carolina, for the copy of *Humorous Folk Tales of the South Carolina Negro*.

To my friend and mentor Professor Henry Louis Gates Jr. for his support, advice and his book *The Annotated African American Folktales*, which inspired this volume.

To my friends and extended family in West Africa, including the griots, who keep the traditions of folklore and history alive through their storytelling.

To the handful of modern-day American griots and professional storytellers who keep the flame alive: Darion McCloud, Carolyn "Jabulile" White, Anita "Aunt Pearlie Sue" Singleton-Prather, Fouchena Sheppard, Elsie White and Minerva King.

To LornaBelle Gethers Coakley for alerting me to the illustration *Decoration Day*, by S.G. McCutcheon.

To Charles Waring of the *Charleston Mercury* for printing a couple of excerpts.

And to Chad Rhoad of Arcadia Publishing and The History Press for his enthusiasm for this project.

African Prologue

I spent the summers of 2022 and 2023 in Togo, Gambia and Senegal, West Africa, and one aspect of these journeys was observing the griot tradition of that region. Traditional cultures had storytellers who provided oral histories and folk tales as a means of preserving their past and passing down lessons of life and history.

In England, the bards and wandering minstrels passed along the stories of King Arthur and Robin Hood; their German counterparts told stories of the Brothers Grimm, what we know today as *Grimm's Fairy Tales*; and the tales of Middle Eastern bards were compiled one thousand years ago as *The Arabian Nights*.

West Africa was no different. For thousands of years, griots (pronounced gree-ohs) recited the histories of the people of their regions and royal lineages and folk tales of instruction. Mamadou Kouyate, a Malian griot, once explained, "We are the memory of mankind." Gambian scholar Hassoum Ceesay added, "Our children, even adults, including leaders, need to be reminded that in Gambian society of yore, adults' fireside chats and stories were meant to entertain and to communicate the values of our society for a healthy living."

I met a number of griots and saw the reverence they are given in West African society. In Dakar, Senegal, they have the baobab tree on the grounds of the Museum of Dakar. This one-thousand-year-old tree is where the griots are traditionally buried. I stopped there to pay my respects to my predecessors as a historian and storyteller. At the National Museum in Banjul, Gambia, I stood in awe of the statue of the griot.

During the last century, writers have documented such griot tales in the literature of Africa. Classics of the genre include *The Sundiata Epic*, the story of a disabled young prince who becomes the king of Mali; *Sona Mariama*, about a Gambian girl who escapes from her abusive father to become a queen of her nation; and the Anansi stories, tales of a wise spider who outwits stronger enemies. But what is particularly interesting is the connection between such tales and the African American culture of South Carolina.

In South Carolina, as in much of the American South, elderly African Americans would often sit on front porches and in other gathering places to repeat tales of historical events they witnessed or lore that was passed down through the generations. Such traditions have largely disappeared in recent years, but what has been documented is quite fascinating. I met a griot in Gambia who told me a tale of an evil chief who sold his own brother to European slave traders. Ironically, the folklorist Edward C.L. Adams recorded a tale from a Black man named Thaddeus Goodson near Columbia in 1928 about "King Buzzard." This was the story of a wicked African chief who sold his brethren to slave traders. God punished him for his avarice by turning him into King Buzzard, who was doomed to wander the Earth for eternity to feast on the remains of the dead.

While visiting the West African Cultural Center in Dakar, Senegal, West Africa, I spoke with Dr. Ousmane Sene, who started the center. He told me that in his youth, the elders of the Wolof people would tell tales of the rabbit known as Leuk and his adventures with Bouki, a Wolof word for "hyena." The rabbit was wise and clever, but Bouki was greedy. In every story, Bouki would lose to Leuk, and the elders would explain to the youth that they should be social and smart like Luek, not greedy and selfish like Bouki. This was an example of how the parents of that region would teach children what was considered ideal behavior.

One of the places I saw in Dakar was the Museum at the University of Dakar. The tour guide Abdul Sey showed my group a drum that was played when Senegal declared its independence from France in 1960 and was no longer a part of French West Africa. Then we were shown the "Talking Drum." When young boys went through their manhood initiation ceremonies, they were taught the secret code of the drum messages, which could be heard throughout the villages. No one other than those who were initiated could know the drum code.

During the days of American slavery, enslavers forbade the playing of drums for fear that they would be used to call the enslaved to arms. After the Stono Slave Rebellion, which occurred near Charleston in 1739 and in which plantations were burned and enslavers were killed, the Negro Act of 1740 banned the use of drums among the Black population of the region.

In 1874, a white Massachusetts writer named Abbie Holmes Christensen documented the stories of a Black man named Prince Baskin from Nathaniel Heyward's plantation in Port Royal. Baskin told stories of his "African granddaddy," who spoke of a smart rabbit that outsmarted a wolf that tried to trap the hare by creating a baby made of tar, similar to the type of tale described by Dr. Sene. This was the foundation of the famous "tar baby" story. Around the same time in Georgia, Joel Chandler Harris recorded a similar story from a Black man known as "Uncle" George Terrell, who was later fictionalized as Uncle Remus.

One tale I heard in Senegal was "The Talking Skull." This was the story of a man who found a skull on the ground and asked, "How did this get here?" The skull replied, "Talk brought me here." The man ran to the village chief and told him of the skull, and the chief threatened to kill the man if he was wasting his time.

The man brought the chief the skull, which refused to talk. The chief beheaded the man, and the skull then said, "You now see how talk brought me here."

This reminded me of the folk tale I was told as a boy of the man who was going to steal the plantation owner's feed from the barn when a nearby mule said, "Look here, don't you steal my feed!" Then the man ran into the plantation owner and told him, "Anything that mule tells you is a doggone lie!"

It was through such stories that I saw the origins of this aspect of the culture of Black South Carolinians.

While my group was in Juffereh Village in Gambia, we spoke with Lamin Ndie, a tour guide of the village. He pointed to a nearby island that was a ten-minute ride by motorboat from their coast, and he told us of the British slave trader who operated on that island in the 1800s. He said that when the British abolished their slave trade, the captain of the slave port received the news. Angered by the impending loss of income, the captain gathered the Africans from the slave pen and told them, "Our king has sent word that there will be no more slavery in this area." The Africans cheered, but the captain added, "However, you are free on only one condition." The captain pointed to the distant shore of the village and said, "Swim back."

Another interesting tale comes from the Gambian village of Bakau. The story goes that some five centuries ago, the child of a female spirit fell into the town's well. Two local brothers rescued the child, and the female spirit rewarded them by stating that anyone who made a prayer by the well would have their wish come true. The spirit also said the brothers' family would forever remain guardians of the well. Today, the well is a pool for crocodiles that is visited by tourists, and the descendants of the brothers are said to have inherited the guardianship of the pool.

Some of the folklore and history of the Gambia appears in a series of pamphlets by the National Centre of Arts and Culture of that nation. One of the included legends is that of Queen Mama Kebereng Jammeh, who ruled during the 1500s. It is said that this queen was so beautiful, one day, a King Demba of the nearby kingdom of Jokadu came to visit her. The queen was bathing, so her servants told him to wait. When she emerged, the king was so struck by her beauty that he was speechless. Queen Jammeh stated, "This king will be my husband if he leaves the throne and gives me control of Jokadu." The king was so smitten that he agreed, and this was how Jokadu was absorbed into the modern-day Gambia.

In Dakar, the capital of nearby Senegal, my group went to the Black Civilizations Museum. A young guide named Khady Ba, who is also majoring in political science at the Cheikh Anta Diop University of Dakar, told us this amazing story. In 1820, some Moors attacked the Senegalese village of Nder. Their queen and her younger sister led their men to a nearby location to treat their wounds, and in their absence, the Moors attacked again. The women realized they were outnumbered, but rather than submit to slavery, they gathered in a hut and set it on fire, preferring to die with dignity. The queen's younger sister Ndatte Yalla Mbodj led raids against the Moors and the French colonizers until her death in 1860. Khady Ba then pointed to a portrait of Queen Mbodj and said with pride, "She is also my great-great-grandmother."

These few stories reflect just a small sample of the fascinating annals of West African history and folklore that is mostly unknown to the American reader.[2]

1

Testimonies from the Attempted Denmark Vesey Rebellion

In 1822, Denmark Vesey, a free Black man in Charleston, South Carolina, was arrested for attempting to organize a major rebellion against slavery. After his trial, its transcript was published as Negro Plot: An Account of the Late Intended Insurrection among a Portion of the Blacks of the City of Charleston, South Carolina *(Boston, MA: Joseph W. Ingraham, 1822). These excerpts are firsthand accounts of that story.*

Even whilst walking through the streets in company with another, He [Denmark Vesey] was not idle; for if his companion bowed to a white person he would rebuke him, and observe that all men were born equal, and that he was surprised that anyone would degrade himself by such conduct; that he would never cringe to the whites, nor ought anyone who had the feelings of a man. When answered, "We are slaves," he would sarcastically and indignantly reply, "You deserve to remain slaves."[3]

The Voluntary confession of ROLLA, to the Court, made after his trial, but before sentence was passed on him.

> I know Denmark Vesey, on one occasion he asked me, "What news?" I told him, "None." He replied, "We are free, but the white people here won't let us be so; and the only way is, to raise up and fight the whites." I went to his house one night, to learn where the meetings were held. I never conversed on this subject with Batteau

or Ned. Vesey told me, he was the leader in this plot. I never conversed either with Peter or Mingo. Vesey induced me to join. When I went to Vesey's house, there was a meeting there, the room was full of people, but none of them white. That night, at Vesey's, we determined to have arms made, and each man to put in twelve and a half cents towards that purpose. Though Vesey's room was full, I did not know one individual there. At this meeting, Vesey said, "We were to take the guardhouse and magazines, to get arms; that we ought to rise up against the whites to get our liberties." He was the first to rise up and speak, and he read to us from the Bible, how the children of Israel were delivered out of Egypt from bondage; he said, that the rising would take place last Sunday night [June 16], and that Peter Poyas was one.[4]

Examination of SALLY, a Negro woman belonging to Mr. Alexander Howard.

I know Jesse, and heard him speak several times about it; one day in particular, he was anxious to see his brother, who has my mother for his wife, and waited until he came, when they conversed together. Jesse said, he had got a horse to go into the country, to bring down men to fight the white people; that he was allowed to pass by two parties of the patrol on the road, but that a third party had brought him back, and that if there were but five men like him, they would destroy the city. This was on last Sunday week [June 16], he said, that before three o'clock, that night, all the white people would be killed. That if any person informed, or would not join in the fight, such person would be killed or poisoned. He frequently came into the yard to see his brother, and I threatened to inform, if he came there, and spoke in that way, to get us all into trouble. We never had any quarrel.[5]

Examination of LOT, a Negro man belonging to Mr. Forrester.

I know Jesse; he met me last Sunday week [June 16] at the corner of Boundary Street, as I was coming into town; he said, he was going to get a horse to go into the country. From what my master had told me the Thursday before, I distrusted his errand, and gave him a caution. When, as I was going down into town towards Mr. Hibben's ferry slip, and conversing with him, he said, "You shall see tonight, when I come down, what I am going up for, and, if my own father does not assist, I will cut off his head[.]" He said, he was going as far as Goose Creek bridge, and would get a horse if it cost him nine dollars. The church bells were then ringing, and at half past eleven o'clock, same day, I saw him at Mr. Howard's, and afterwards understood from Sally, that he had set off for the country, and had been brought back by the patrol.[6]

Examination of FRANK, a Negro man belonging to Mrs. Ferguson.

I know Denmark Vesey, and have been to his house; I have heard him say, that the negro's situation was so bad, he did not know how they could endure it; and was astonished they did not rise and fight for themselves, and he advised me to join, and rise. He said, he was going about to see different people, and mentioned the names of Ned Bennett and Peter Poyas, as concerned with him; that he had spoken to Ned and Peter on this subject, and that they were to go about and tell the blacks, that they were free, and must rise and fight for themselves: that they would take the magazines and guardhouses, and the city, and be free; that he was going to send into the country to inform the people there, too; he said, he wanted me to join them. I said, I could not answer. He said, if I would not go into the country for him, he could get others; he said, himself, Ned Bennett, Peter Poyas, and Monday Gell, were the principal men, and himself the head man. He said, they were the principal men to go about and inform the people, and fix them, &c. that one party would land on South Bay, one about Wappoo and about the farms; that the party which was to land on South Bay, was to take the guardhouse, and get arms, and then they would be able to go on; that the attack was to commence about twelve o'clock at night; that great numbers would come from all about, and it must succeed, as so many were engaged in it; that they would kill all the whites; that they would leave their masters' houses, and assemble near the lines, march down and meet the party which would land on South Bay; that he was going to send a man into the country on a horse, to bring down the country people, and that he would pay for the horse. He gave two dollars to Jesse, to get the horse on Saturday week last [June 15], about one o'clock in the day, and myself and witness (No. 8,) also put in 25 cents apiece, and he told Jesse, if he could not go, he must send someone else. I have seen Ned Bennett at Vesey's. I one night met at Vesey's a great number of men, and as they came in, they each handed him some money. Vesey said, there was a little man, named Jack, who could not be killed, and who would furnish them with arms; he had a charm, and would lead them; that Charles Drayton had promised to be engaged with them. Vesey said, the negroes were living such an abominable life, they ought to rise. I said, I was living well. He said, though I was, others was not, and that it was such fools as I, that were in their way, and would not help them, and that, after all things were well, he would mark me. He said, he did not go with Creighton to Africa, because he had not a will, he wanted to stay and see what he could do for his fellow creatures. I met Ned, Monday, and others, at Denmark Vesey's, where they were talking about this business.

The first time I spoke with Monday Gell, it was one night at Denmark Vesey's house, where I heard Vesey tell Monday, that he must send someone into the country to bring the people down. Monday said, he had sent up Jack, and told him to tell the people to come down and join in the fight against the whites; and also to ascertain and inform him how many people he could get. A few days after, I met Vesey, Monday, and Jack in the streets, under Mr. Duncan's trees, at night, where Jack stated, he had been into the country, 'round by Goose Creek and Dorchester; that he had spoken to 6,600 persons, who had agreed to join. Monday said to Vesey, that if Jack had so many men, they had better wait no longer, but begin the business at once, and others would join. The first time I saw Monday at Vesey's, he was going away early, when Vesey asked him to stay, to which Monday replied, he expected that night a meeting at his house, to fix upon and mature the plan, &c. and that he could stay no longer. I afterwards conversed with Monday in his shop, when he asked me, if I had heard that Bennett's and Poyas's people were taken up, that it was a great pity. He said, he had joined in the business. I told him to take care he was not taken up. Whenever I talked with Vesey, he always spoke of Monday Gell as being his principal and active man in this business.[7]

Confession of JESSE, the slave of Thomas Blackwood, Esqr.; furnished to the Court by the Rev. Dr. D. HALL.

I was invited to Denmark Vesey's house, and when I went, I found several men met together, among whom was Ned Bennett, Peter Poyas, and others, whom I did not know. Denmark opened the meeting by saying, he had an important secret to communicate to us, which we must not disclose to anyone, and if we did, we should be put to instant death. He said, we were deprived of our rights and privileges by the white people, and that our church was shut up, so that we could not use it, and that it was high time for us to seek for our rights, and that we were fully able to conquer the whites, if we were only unanimous and courageous, as the St. Domingo people were. He then proceeded to explain his plan, by saying, that they intended to make the attack by setting the governor's mills on fire, and also some houses near the water, and as soon as the bells began to ring for fire, that they should kill every man, as he came out of his door, and that the servants in the yards should do it, and that it should be done with axes and clubs, and afterwards they should murder the women and children, for he said, God had so commanded it in the scriptures. At another meeting at Denmark's, Ned Bennett and Peter Poyas, and several others were present in conversation, some said, they thought it was cruel to kill the ministers, and the women and children, but Denmark Vesey said, he thought it was for our safety, not to spare one white skin alive, for this was the plan they pursued in St. Domingo. He then said to me, "Jesse, I want you to go into the country, to enlist as many of the country negroes as possible, to be in readiness to come down to assist us." I told him, I had no horse, and no money to hire one; he then took out two dollars, and gave them to me to hire a horse, and told me pass them without being taken up; so I returned, and told Denmark, at which he expressed his sorrow, and said, the business was urgent, for they wanted the country people to be armed, that they might attack the forts at the same time, and also to take every ship and vessel in the harbor, and to put every man to death, except the captains. For, said he, it will not be safe to stay in Charleston, for as soon as they had got all the money out of the banks, and the goods out of the stores on board, they intended to sail for St. Domingo; for he had a promise, that they would receive and protect them. This Jesse asserted to me was the truth, whilst the tears were running down his cheeks, and he appeared truly penitent; and I have reason to hope, that he obtained pardon from God, through the merits of Christ, and was prepared to meet his fate with confidence, and that he was accepted of God. At four o'clock in the morning of the execution, I visited all the prisoners condemned, and found Jesse at prayers. He told me, his mind was placid and calm; he then assured me, that what he had told me was the truth, and that he was prepared to meet his God to enlist as many as possible.[8]

Confession of MONDAY GELL.

I come out as a man who knows he is about to die—sometime after Christmas, Vesey passed my door, he called in, said to me that he was trying to gather the blacks to try and see if anything could be done to overcome the whites; he asked me to join; I asked him his plan and his numbers; he said he had Peter Poyas, Ned Bennet, and Jack Purcell; he asked me to join; I said no; he left me and I saw him not for some time. About four or five weeks ago as I went up Wentworth Street, Frank Ferguson met me, and said he had four plantations of people who he was to go for on Saturday, 15th June. How, said I, will you bring them down; he said through the woods; he asked me if I was going towards Vesey's to ask Vesey to be at home that evening, and he would be there to tell him his success. I asked Jack Purcell to carry this message, he said he would; that same evening at my house I met Vesey's mulatto boy, he told me Vesey wished to see me, I went with him; when I went into Vesey's I met Ned Bennett, Peter Poyas, and Frank Ferguson, and Adam, and Gullah Jack; they were consulting about the plan; Frank told Vesey on Saturday 15th, he would go and bring down the people and lodge them near town in the woods; the plan was to arm themselves by breaking open the stores with arms. I then told Vesey I would join them, after some time I told them I had some business of my own and asked them to excuse me, I went away, and only then was I ever there. One evening Perault Strohecker, and Bacchus Hammett brought to my shop a keg, and asked me to let it stay there till they sent for it; I said yes, but did not know the contents; the next evening Gullah Jack came and took away the keg, this was since I have been in prison I learnt that the keg contained powder.

Pharo Thompson is concerned, and he told me, a day or two after Ned and Peter were taken up, if he could get a fifty dollar bill, he would run away; about two Sundays before I was brought here, he asked me, in Archdale street, "When shall we be like those white people in the church?" I said when it pleased God; Sunday before I was taken up, he met me as I came out of Archdale church, and took me into a stable in said street, and told me he had told his master, who had asked him, that he had nothing to do in this affair; which was a lie. William Colcock came to my shop once and said a brother told him that five hundred men were making up for the same purpose. Frank said he was to send to Hell Hole swamp to get men.

Perault Strohecker is engaged; he used to go of a Sunday on horseback up the road to a man he knows on the same errand. One Sunday he asked me to go with him; I went and Smart Anderson; we went to a small house a little way from the road after you turn into the shipyard road, on its left hand; they two went into the stable with an old man that lived there, I remained in the yard; they remained in the stable about half an hour; as soon as they came out, I and Perault started to town to go to church, and left Smart there; I was told by Denbow Martin, who has a wife in Mr. Smith's house, that Stephen Smith belonged to some of the gangs.

Saby Gaillard is concerned; he met me on the Bay, before the 16th of June and gave me a piece of paper from his pocket; this paper was about the battle that Boyer had in St. Domingo; in a day or two he called on me and asked if I had read it, and said if he had as many men he would do the same too, as he could whip ten white men himself; he frequently came to me to speak about this matter, and at last I had to insult him out of the shop; he and Paris Ball was often together. A week before I was taken up, Paris told me that my name was called.

Morris Brown [pastor of Hampstead African Church, where Vesey attended] knew nothing of it, and we agreed not to let him, Harry Drayton, or Charles Corr, know anything about it. ———— told me in my store that he was to get some powder from his master and give it to Peter Poyas; he seemed to have been a long time engaged in it, and to know a great deal. Joe Jore acknowledged to me once or twice that he had joined, he said he knew some of the Frenchmen concerned; he knew I was in it before the 16th June.[9]

After he was found guilty, Vesey was hanged with a number of his followers in Charleston on July 2, 1822.

2

Stories of Slavery

Most of the stories that follow are from the Works Progress Administration's Federal Slave Narratives Project that was conducted from 1936 to 1937. Writers, most of whom were from southern states, interviewed elderly survivors of slavery for their accounts. A handful of Black interviewers, such as Augustus Ladson, worked in South Carolina, but most often, white interviewers recorded these stories, not considering that Black people raised in slavery were more likely to be candid with other Black people. Many of these stories have been edited for clarity, as most used a strong dialect, and length.

"BURNT PILGRIM"

An Intriguing Tale of Resistance Against the Ku Klux Klan

When I was a boy on the Gilmore place, the Ku Klux would come along at night a riding the niggers like they was goats. Yes sir, they had them down on all fours a crawling, and they would be on their backs. They would carry the niggers to Turk Creek bridge and make them set up on the bannisters of the bridge; then they would shoot them off of the bannisters into the water. I declare them was the most awful days I ever saw. A darky name Sam Scaife drifted a hundred yards in the water downstream. His folks took and got him out of that bloody water and buried him on the bank of the creek. The Ku Klux would not let them take him to no graveyard. Fact is, they would not let many of the niggers take de dead bodies of the folks nowhere. They just throwed them in a big hole right there and pulled some dirt over them. For weeks after that, you could not go near that place, because it stink so far and bad. Sam's folks, they throwed a lot of "Indian-head" rocks all over his grave, because it was so shallow, and them rocks kept the wild animals from a bothering Sam. You can still see them rocks, I could carry you there right now.

Another darky, Eli McCollum, floated about three and a half miles down de creek. His folks went there and took him out and buried him on the banks of the stream right by the side of a Indian mound. You can see that Indian mound to dis very day. It is big as my house is, over there on the Chester side.

The Ku Klux and the niggers fought at New Hope Church. A big rock marks the spot today. The church, it done burnt down. The big rock sets about seven miles east of Lockhart on the road to Chester. De darkies killed some of de Ku Klux and they took their dead and put them in Pilgrims Church. Then they set fire to that church and it burnt everything up to the very bones of the white folks. And ever since then, that spot has been known as "Burnt Pilgrim." The darkies left most of the folks right there for the buzzards and other wild things to eat up. Because them niggers had to get away from there; and they didn't have no time for to fetch no word or nothing to no folks at home. They had a hiding place not fer from "Burnt Pilgrim." A darky name Austin Sanders, he was carrying some victuals to his son. The Ku Klux caught him and they asked him where he was going. He allowed that he was a setting some bait fer coons. The Ku Klux took and shot him and left him lying right in de middle of de road with a biscuit in his dead mouth.

—Bradley Gilmore, Union, South Carolina[10]

TALES OF THE OLD SLAVE MARKET IN CHARLESTON

From "Stories Collected from Slaves," a manuscript from Leonarda J. Aimar, completed in 1926. This story was dictated by William Pinckney on October 16, 1917.

My father was Cato Pinckney, and he belonged to Otis Miller. My mother was Maria Pinckney, née Atkins. She belonged to James English. I was born October 16, 1830, on South Battery in Charleston, South Carolina, in front of Legare Street. The Wilkinsons live in the house now. I am the father of 13 children, 8 of which are living now. Kate Pinckney is my wife.

Mr. English's daughter married Shingler. I went to her. I served Colonel Shingler from the time the first gun was fired in the war. I was in three battles: Manassas, Petersburg and one in Maryland. I was present with my master when Lee surrendered to Grant. I suffered through cold and famine during the war. I was never sold in slavery and stayed with Colonel Shingler until he died. After his death, I worked for N.A. Hunt ten years and six months; then I came to Charles P. Aimar and have been forty-three years in the service of the Aimar family.

I remember Melchier Garner, who married Miss Ann Smith, daughter of Thomas Ridgen Smith. He wore knee breeches and kept a jewelry store. I also remember the firm of Howard and Vincent. They belonged to the Scotch company which held its meeting in Hibernian Hall. Cabmas was the captain of the company. I also remember some members of the Jockey Club, which were Townsend, Whaley and Bailey. Some of the slave traders were McBride, Ryan, Hume, Silinus, Mordecai, Gilchrist, Oaks, Max Levy, Luther, White, Marshall and Wriggs.

The slave market on Chalmers Street, one door from State Street, Charleston, South Carolina. The traders would put the slaves on the table and tell their age by their teeth. Adger's House on the Southeast Corner of Calhoun Street and Ashley Avenue was built by Thomas Ryan, a slave trader. The slaves to be sold were locked in the outhouses which are standing now. Thackett did the bidding. A coachman would bring $1,700. In January, many slaves would be lost to their owners by their masters betting on the races, often one or two plantations would be staked. Slaves would be traded to Georgia, Mobile, Mississippi and New Orleans. The biggest slave trading places were in New Orleans and Atlanta. A slave would often serve three masters; if he ran away his master would sell him, and so on.

The Sugar House was on the corner of Magazine and Legare Streets; next door to the Old Roper Hospital. A grocery store stands on the site now. If a slave ran away or misbehaved, he would be put there to be sold or punished. One form of punishment was treading the wheel. If the slave fell off, he broke his leg. The law allowed five paddle strokes and five cowhides. The slave was made to take off his clothes and struck anywhere. A good many died from the effects of whipping. Stocks were also used as a form of punishment, sometimes the slaves died in stocks.

—William Pinckney, Charleston, South Carolina[11]

EYEWITNESS ACCOUNT FROM
THE CHARLESTON SLAVE MARKET

I visited the slave pens, the auction rooms in which the bodies and souls of men, women, and children had been knocked down to the highest bidder. The dealers set up their mart in a reputable quarter, within a stone throw of St. Michael's Church, close by the guard house, the Registry of Deeds, the Theological Library, Sunday School Depository, and the courthouse. A shell had burst in the courtroom, another had opened the entire front of the Sunday School Depository. I entered the Theological Library through an opening made by a shell, and stood amid a pile of sermons, tracts, magazines and papers, turning to pulp beneath the rain, which had full access through the shattered roof.

Amid such surroundings stood the Central Mart—a building with a massive iron gate opening to a large room, flanked on one side by a long table, upon which, on auction days, the slaves stood for inspection and sale, to be handled, felt of, as cows and pigs are handled at a country auction.

Adjoining the sale hall was a room used for the inspection of women; where, disrobed in part of their clothing, they were exposed to the gaze of lascivious men. Beyond was the prison, with iron-grated cells, and a yard surrounded by high walls, in which the slaves were exercised while waiting for the day of sale.

A colored woman, Dinah Moore, entered the building.

"I was sold here two years ago," she said.

"You never will be sold again; you are free now," my reply.

"Thank God! Oh, the blessed Jesus he has heard my prayer! I am so glad; only I wish I could see my husband. He was sold at the same time into the country, and has gone I don't know where."[12]

THOMAS GOODWATER INTERVIEW

I come from Mount Pleasant and was born January 15, 1855, on Mr. Lias Winning plantation on the Cooper River. I was then six years ole when the war broke out and could remember a good many things. My ma and pa been named Angeline and Thomas Goodwater who had eight boys and eight gals. I use to help my grandma around the kitchen, who was the cook for the family. I am the older of the two who is alive. Peter, the one alive, live on my place now, but I ain't hear from them for two years. I don't know for certain that he's alive or not.

In slavery the people use to go and catch possums and rabbits so as to have meat to eat. The driver used to shoot cows an in the night the slaves go and skin them and issue them around to all the slaves, especially when cows come from another plantation. He go around and tell the slaves they better go and get some fish before all go. Any time anyone say he have fish, it was understood he mean cow meat. Our boss ain't never catch on nor did he ever miss any cow; Guy Simmons, the colored driver, was under Sam Black, the white overseer. Sam Black wasn't mean, he just had to carry out orders of Lias Winning, our master. There was a vegetable garden that had things for the year round so we could have soup and soup could be in the Big House.

One day when I was about fourteen, I did something and ma didn't like it. A bunch of gals been home and ma wheeled my shirt over my head and start to beat me right before the gals. They begged her not to lick [beat] me and she got mad just for that. I couldn't help myself 'cause she tied the shirt over my head with a string, my hands and all was tied in the shirt with the string. In hot weather, gals an' boys go in their undershirts and nothing else.

Boys in dose days could fight but couldn't throw anyone on the ground. We had to stand up and either beat or get beat.

I was married in 1872 to Catharine, my wife. At our wedding we had plenty to eat. There was possums, wine, cake, and plenty of fruits. I had on a black suit, black shoes, white tie and shirt. Catharine had on all white. I stay with Catharine's people for a year 'til I was able to build on my land. I am a father of nineteen children; ten boys and nine gals; only two now living.

Lias Venning wasn't a mean man. He couldn't lick pa because they grew up together or at least he didn' try. But he liked his woman slaves. One day, ma was in the field working alone and he went there and tried to rape her. Ma pulled his ears almost off, so he let her off and gone and tell pa he better talk to ma. Pa was working in the salt pen an' when Mr. Venning tell him, he just laughed because 'e know why ma did it.

There was a family doctor on the plantation name James Hibbins. My eye use to run water a lot and he took out my eye and couldn't put it back in, that's why I am blind now. He ask ma an' pa not to say anything about it because he'd lose his job an' have his license take 'way. So ma an' pa even didn't say anything even to Mr. Venning as to the truth of my blindness.

I was by the "nigger quarters" one day when Blake, the overseer, start to lick a slave. She take the whip from him and closed the door and give him a snake beating.

Our boss had about three hundred acres of land and over a hundred slaves. The overseer never woke the slaves. They could go in the field any time in the morning because everybody was given their task work on Monday morning. Nobody never worked when it rained or was cold. Nothing make Lias Venning so mad as when one would steal; it make him good and mad. Any one he catch stealing was sure to get a good whipping. He didn't like for anyone to fight either.

They tell me that when slaves was shipped to New Orleans they had to be dress up in nice clothes. My pa could read and write because he lived in the city here. His missus teach him.

Isaac Wigfall run away and went to Florida and met a white man on a horse with a gun. He asked the man for a piece of tobacco. The man gave him the gun to hold while he got the tobacco for him. Isaac take the gun and point it at the man and asked him, "You know what in dis gun?" The man got frightened and he told the man, "You better be gone or I'll empty it in you." The man gone and come back with a group of men and hound dogs. He'd just make it to the river before the dogs catch him. He had a piece of light wood knot and every time a dog got near, he hit him on the neck and killed all of them. The men went back to get more help and dogs but when they got back, Isaac was gone.

There used to be dances almost every week and the older boys and gals walk twelve miles dis to be there. Sometime there was a tambourine beater, sometimes they used ole wash tubs and beat it wood sticks, and sometimes they just clap their hands. When anyone died, they was buried in the morning or early afternoon.[13]

INTERVIEW WITH HENRY BROWN

I was nicknamed during the days of slavery. My name was Henry but they call me Toby. My sister, Josephine, too was nickname an' call Jesse. Our mistress had a cousin by that name. My oldest brother was a sergeant on the Charleston Police Force around 1868. I had two other sister, Louise and Rebecca.

My first owner was Arthur Barnwell Rose. Then Colonel A.G. Rhodes bought the plantation who sol' it to Captain Frederick W. Wagener. James Sottile then got in possession who sol' it to the DeCostas, and a few weeks ago Mrs. Albert Callitin Simms, who I'm told is a former member of Congress, bought it. Now I'm wondering if she is going to let me stay. I hope so because I'm old now and can't work.

My pa was named Abraham Brown; he was born on Coals Island in Beaufort County. Colonel Rhodes bought him for his driver, then he move here. I didn't know much 'bout him; he didn't live so long after slavery 'cause he was old.

Colonel Rhodes had a son and a daughter. The son went back to England after his death and the daughter went to Germany with her husband. They ain't never come back so the place was sold for tax.

During the war we was carry to Deer Pond, twelve miles on this side of Columbia. When the war was end pa brought my sister, Louise, Rebecca, who was too small to work, Josephine an' me home. All my people is long lifted. My grand pa and grand ma on pa side come right from Africa. They was stolen and brought here. They used to tell us of how white men had pretty cloth on boats which they was to exchange for some of their ornament. When they take the ornament to the boat they was carry way down to the bottom an' was locked in. They was anchored on or near Sullivan's Island where they been feed like dogs. A big pot was use for cooking. In that pot peas was cooked and left to cool. Everybody went to the pot with the hands and all eat from the pot.

I was born two years before the war an' was seven when it end. That was in 1857. I never went to school but five months in my life, but could learn easy. Very seldom I had to be told to do the same thing twice.

The slaves had a plenty of vegetables all the time. Master planted three acres just for the slaves which was attended to in the mornings before task time. All provision was made as to the distribution on Monday evenings after task.

My master had two place: one on Big Island an' on Coals Island in Beaufort County. He didn't have any overseer. My pa was his driver.

Pa say this place was given to Mr. Rhodes with a thousand acres of land by England. But it dwindled to thirty-five when the other was taken back by England.

There wasn't but ten slaves on this plantation. The driver call the slaves at four so they could git their breakfast. They always work the garden first and at seven go in the corn and cotton field. Some finish their task by twelve an' others worked 'til seven but had the task to finish. No one was whipped unless he needed it; no one else could whip master's slaves. He wouldn't stand for it. We had it better then than now because white men lynch an' burn now an' do other things they couldn't do then. They shoot you down like dogs now, an' nothing said or done.

No slave was supposed to be whipped in Charleston except at the Sugar House. There was a jail for whites, but if a slave ran away an' got there he could disown his master an' the state wouldn't let him take you.

All colored people has to have a pass when they went traveling; free as well as slaves. If one didn't the patrollers, who was hired by rich white men would give you a good whipping an' send you back home. My pa didn't need any one to write his pass 'cause he could write as well as master. How he got his education, I didn't know.

Saturday was a working day but the task was much shorter than other days. Men didn't have time to frolic because they had to find food for the family; master never give enough to last the whole week. A peck o' corn, three pound o' bacon, quart o' molasses, a quart o' salt, an' a pack o' tobacco was given the men. The wife got the same thing but children according to age. Only one holiday slaves had an' that was Christmas.

Cornshucking parties was conducted by a group of farmers who take their slaves or send them to the neighboring ones 'til all the corn was shuck. Each one would furnish food enough for all slaves at his party. Some use to have nothing but bake potatoes and some kind of vegetable.

An unmarried young man was call a half-hand. When he want to marry he just went to master an' say there's a gal he would like to have for wife. Master would say yes and that night more chicken would be fry and everything eatable would be prepare at master expense. The couple went home after the supper, without any reading of matrimony, man and wife.

A man once married his ma and didn't know it. He was sell from her when 'bout eight years old. When he grow to a young men, slavery then was over, he met this woman who he like and so they were married. They was married a month when one night they started to tell of their experiences an' how many times they was sol'. The husband told how he was sold from his mother who liked him dearly. He told how his ma faint when they took him away and how his master then use to brand his baby slaves at a year old. When he showed her the brand, she faint because she then realize that she had married her son.

Slaves didn't have to use their own remedy for sickness for good doctors been hired to look at them. There was, as is, though, some weed use for fever an' headache as: blacksnake root, furry work, jimpson weed, one that tie on the head which bring sweat from you like hail, an' hickory leaf. If the hickory is keep on the head too long it will blister it.

When the war was fighting the white men burn the bridge at the foot of Spring Street so the Yankees couldn't get over but they built pontoons while some make the horses swim 'cross. One night while at Deer Pond, I hear something like thunder until about eleven the next day. When the thing I thought was thunder stop, master tell us that evening we was free. I wasn't surprise to know for as little as I was I know the Yankees was going' to free us with the help of God.

I was married twice, an' had two gals an' a boy with firs' wife. I have three boys with the second; the youngest is just eight.

Lincoln did jus' what God intended him to do, but I think nothing 'bout Calhoun on account of what he say in one of his speech 'bout colored people. He said: "Keep the niggers down."

To see colored boys going around now with paper an' pencil in their hands don't look real to me. During slavery he would be whipped 'til not a skin was left on his body.

My pa was a preacher why I become a Christian so early; he preach on the plantation to the slaves. On Sunday the slaves went to the white church. He use to tell us of hell an' how hot it is. I was so afraid of hell 'til I was always trying to do the right thing so I couldn't go to that terrible place.

I don't care about this world and its vanities because the Great Day is coming when I shall lay down an' my stammering tongue going to lie silent in my head. I want a house not made with hands but eternal in the Heavens. That Man up there, is all I need; I'm going to still trust Him. Before the coming of Christ, men was kill for His name sake; today they curse Him. It's nearly time for the world to come to and for He said, "'Bout two thousand years I shall come again," and that time is fast approaching.[14]

SUSAN HAMILTON'S TALE OF HER FATHER

My pa belong to a man on Edisto Island. From what he said, his master was very mean. Pa real name was Adam Collins but he took his master name; he was de coachman. Pa did something one day and his master whipped him. The next day, which was Monday, pa carry him about four miles from home in the woods and give him the same amount of licking [beating] he was given on Sunday. He tied him to a tree and unhitched the horse so it couldn't git tie up and kill himself. Pa then gone to de landing and catch a boat that was coming to Charleston with farm products. He [was] permitted by his master to go to town on errands, which helped him to go on the boat without being questioned. When he got here, he gone on the waterfront and asked for a job on a ship so he could get to the North. He got the job and sailed with the ship. They searched the island up and down for him with hound dogs and when it was thought he was drowned, 'cause they track him to the river, did they give up. One of his master's friends gone to New York and went in a store where pa was employed as a clerk. He recognized pa as easy as pa recognize him. He gone back home and tell pa's master who knew then that pa wasn't coming back and before he died, he signed papers that pa was free. Pa's ma was dead and he come down to bury her by the permission of his master son who had promised no harm would come to him, but they was fixing plans to keep him, so he went to de Work House and ask to be sold because any slave could sell himself if he could get to de Work House. But it was on record down there so they couldn't sell him and told him his master people couldn't hold him a slave.[15]

INTERVIEW WITH ELIJAH GREEN

I was born in Charleston at 82 King Street, December 25, 1843. The house is still there whose recent owner is Judge Whaley. My ma an' pa was Kate and John Green. My ma had seven children [boys] and I am the last of them. Their names was: Henry, Scipio, Ellis, Nathaniel, Hobart, Mikell and myself.

From the southeast of Calhoun Street, which was then Boundary Street, to the Battery was the city limit an' from the northwest of Boundary Street for several miles was nothing but farmland. All my brothers was farmhands for our master, George W. Jones. I did all the housework 'til the war when I was given to Mr. Wm. Jones's son, Wm. H. Jones as his "daily give servant" who duty was to clean his boots, shoes, sword and make his coffee. He was first lieutenant of the South Carolina Company Regiment. Being his servant, I wear all his cast-off clothes, which I was glad to have. My shoes was call brogan that has brass on the toe. When a slave had one of them, you couldn't tell them he wasn't dress to death.

As the "daily give servant" of Mr. Wm. H. Jones, I had to go to Virginia during the war. In the battle at Richmond General Lee had General Grant almost beaten. He drive him almost in the Potomac River, and then take seven pieces of his artillery. When General Grant see how near defeat he was, he put up a white flag as a signal for timeout to bury his dead.

That flag stay up for three weeks while General Grant was digging trenches. In the meantime he get message to President Lincoln asking him to send a reinforcement of soldiers. General Sherman was in charge of the regiment who send word to General Grant to hold his position 'til he had captured Columbia, Savannah, burned out Charleston while on his way with dispatch of forty-five thousand men. When General Sherman got to Virginia, the battle was renewed and continued for seven days at the end of which General Lee surrendered to General Grant. During the seven days fight the battle got so hot 'til Mr. William Jones made his escape, and it was two days before I know he was gone. One of the generals sent me home an' I got here two days 'fore Mr. William got home. He went up in the attic and stayed there 'til the war was ended. I carry all his meals to him and tell him all the news. Master show was a frightened man; I was sorry for him.

That battle at Richmond, Virginia, was the worst in American history. Dr. George W. Jones, my master, ran a blockade. He had ships roaming the sea to capture pirate ships. He had a daughter, Ellen, who was always kind to the slaves. Master had a driver, William Jenkins, and an overseer, Henry Brown. Both was white. The driver see that the work was done by the supervision of the overseer. Master's farm amounted to twenty-five acres with about eighteen slaves. The overseer blow the horn, which was a conch shell, at six in the morning and every slave better answer when the roll was call at seven. The slaves didn't have to work on Saturday.

Mr. [Thomas] Ryan had a private jail on Queen Street near the Planters Hotel. He was very cruel; he'd lick his slaves to death. Very seldom one of his slaves survive a whipping. He was the opposite to Governor [William] Aiken, who lived on the northwest corner of Elizabeth and Judith Streets. He had several rice plantations, hundreds of his slaves he didn't know.

Not 'til John C. Calhoun body was carried down Boundary Street was the name changed in his honor. He is bury in St. Phillip Church yard, across the street with a laurel tree planted at his head. Four men and me dig his grave an' I cleared the spot where his monument now stands. The monument was put up by Pat Callington, a Charleston mason. I never did like Calhoun because he hated the Negro; no man was ever hated as much as him by a group of people.

The Work House [Sugar House] was on Magazine Street, built by Mr. Columbus C. Trumbone. On Chalmers Street is the slave market from which slaves was taken to Vendue Range and auctioned off. At the foot of Lawrence Street, opposite East Bay Street, on the other side of the trolley tracks is where Mr. Alonzo White kept an' sell slaves from his kitchen. He was a slave broker who had a house that extended almost to the train tracks, which is about three hundred yards going to the waterfront.

No train or trolley tracks was there then, because there was only one railroad here, the Southern, an' the depot was on Ann Street where the Bagging Mill now is.

When slaves run away an' their masters catch them, to the stockade they go where they'd be whipped every other week for a number of mornings. And for God sake don't you be caught with pencil an' paper, that was a major crime. You might as well had kill your master or missus.

One song I know I use to sing to the slaves when master went away, but I wouldn't be so fool as to let him hear me. What I kin 'member of it is:

> *Master gone away*
> *But darkies stay at home,*
> *The year of jubilee is come*
> *And freedom will begun.*

A group of white men was in Doctor Wilson drugstore one day when I went to buy something. They commence to ask me questions concerning some historical happenings and I answer them all. So Dr. Wilson bet me that I couldn't tell who fired the firs' shot on Fort Sumter. I tell him I did know an' he offers a dollar if I was right. I tell him I wasn't going to tell 'less the dollar was given to one of the men. He did so and I told them it was Edward Ruffin who fired the first shot an' the dollar was mine. Anderson was determine not to leave the fort but when 'bout four shells had hit the fort he was glad to be able to come out. When Sherman was coming through Columbia, he fired an' a shell lodged in the South-East and if the State House which was forbidden to be fix. He was coming down Main Street when that happens.

The first two people that was hung in Charleston was Harry and Janie; husband and wife who was slaves of Mr. Christopher Black. Mr. Black had them whipped and they planned to kill the whole family. They poison the breakfast one morning and if two of the family hadn't been asleep, they would have been dead. The others die almost instantly. An investigation was made an' the poison discovered and the two slaves hung on the big oak in the middle of Ashley Avenue.

Slaves was always bury in the night as no one could stop to do it in the day. Old boards was used to make the coffin that was blackened with shoe polish.

After the war I did garden work. Mr. Stiles Bee on James Island give track of land to the Negroes for a school jus' after the war; he put up a shed-like building with a few chairs in it. It was at the place call Cut Bridge.

I was janitor at Benedict College in Columbia for two years and at Claflin in Orangeburg for twelve. The presidents under which I worked was: Allen Webster, grandson of the dictionary maker; J.C. Cook; and Dr. Duntin.

Now all that is passed an I'm living from hand to mouth. The banks took all my money an' I can't work. I do the collecting for my landlord and he give me a room free. If it wasn't for that I don't know what I'd do.[16]

The Charleston novelist Josephine Humphreys alerted this author to a treasure trove of newspaper articles about Mr. Green. It turns out that he was quite the local celebrity as a storyteller in his old age. In 1940, he went to the Charleston News and Courier *to sit down and regale its writers with his tales, which they preserved in the January 5, 1940 edition. The next year, the local artist Elizabeth O'Neill Verner wrote down some of his anecdotes for her book* Mellowed by Time: A Charleston Notebook, *which is available in the reference room at the Charleston County Library. In 1942, local Black women honored him at the old YWCA on 106 Coming Street by inviting him to a program to tell of his adventures at the age of 104!*

This legendary sage died three years later at his home on 7-B Marsh Street of natural causes after refusing to go to a hospital. It is because writers of the time wrote down the stories of such men and women that we know what it was like to have lived through slavery.

DANIEL GODDARD, EX-SLAVE,
SEVENTY-FOUR YEARS OLD

Editor's note: In the following narrative, Mr. Goddard is referring to the Madison Washington Slave Rebellion aboard the ship Creole *in 1841, which resulted in what is described here, as well as the* Amistad *Rebellion of 1839, in which Africans commanded a slave ship. This shows that news of such rebellions traveled among the Black population despite efforts to suppress such stories to prevent a repetition of these events.*

My name is Daniel Goddard. I was born in Columbia, South Carolina, February 14, 1863, to slave parents. You know I recall no contacts I made in slavery, for I was too young during that period. You know, too, if I had been born in Massachusetts, for example, I should have been free, because all slaves in the United States had been set free when President Lincoln, shortly before my birth, January 1863, struck the shackles from bondage.

The Confederate states had seceded from the Union and they paid no attention to the freedom proclamation during the war. So the slaves in the South, generally speaking, stayed on until the Confederacy collapsed in April 1865, and even then, some of the slaves were slow to strike out for themselves, until the federal government made ample preparations to take care of them.

Now you ask, if I heard about escapes of slaves. Sure I did and I heard my parents discuss the efforts of slaves to shake off the shackles. This was probably true because my father's brother, Thomas, was a member of the slave ship which was taking him and 134 others from Virginia to New Orleans. A few miles south of Charleston, the slaves revolted, put the officers and crew in irons, and ran the ship to Nassau.

There they went ashore and the British government refused to surrender them. They settled in the Bahama Islands and some of their descendants are there today. That was about 1830, I think, because my Uncle Thomas was far older than my father. I heard about the other slave revolts, where that African prince, one of a large number of slaves that were kidnaped, took over the Spanish ship *L'Amada*, killing two of the officers. The remaining officers promised to return the slaves to Africa but slyly turned the ship to port in Connecticut. There the Spanish minister at Washington demanded the slaves, as pirates. Appeal was made to the courts and the United States Court ruled that slavery was not legal in Spain and declared the slaves free.

The Nat Turner insurrection in Virginia and the Vesey uprising in Charleston was discussed often, in my presence, by my parents and friends. I learned that revolts of slaves in Martinique, Antigua, Santiago, Caracas and Tortugus, was known all over the South. Slaves were about as well aware of what was going on, as their masters were. However, the masters made it harder for their slaves for a while.

I have a clipping, now worn yellow with age, which says the federal census of 1860, showed there were 487,970 free Negroes and 3,952,760 slaves in the United States at that time. I am not at all surprised at the number of free Negroes. Many South Carolina families freed a number of their slaves. Some slaves had the luck to be able to buy their freedom and many others escaped to free areas. The problem of slavery as a rule, was a question of wits, the slave to escape and the master to keep him from escaping.

I once talked with Frederick Douglass, perhaps the most eminent Negro to appear so far in America. He told me he was born a slave in Maryland, in 1817, and that he served there as a slave for ten years. He escaped to Massachusetts, where he was aided in education and employment by the Garrisons and other abolitionists, and became a leader of his race. He was United States minister to Haiti at the time I met him and was eminent as an orator. He died in 1895.

You ask, what do I think of the presidents. Well, I have always been such an admirer of Andrew Jackson, a South Carolinian, that I may be prejudiced a little. The reason I admire him so much, is because he stood for the Union, and he didn't mean maybe, when he said it. He served his time and God took him, just as he took Moses.

Then Lincoln was raised up for a specific purpose, to end slavery, which was a menace to both whites and Blacks, as I see it. And President Wilson kept the faith of the fathers, when he decided to put the German kaiser where he could no longer throw the world into discord. But there has only been one president whose heart was touched by the cry of distress of the poor and needy and his name is Franklin D. Roosevelt. He is one white man who has turned the bias of the Negroes from the bait of partisan politics.

Yes, sir, I recall the Reconstruction period here in Columbia. My parents lived until I was about grown and we kept the middle of the road, in the matter of selling out to the federal soldiers and carpetbaggers on the one hand, or to designing politicians on the other. But my father was an admirer of General Hampton, because General Hampton owned many Negroes at one time and had treated them well. Between Hampton and Chamberlain for governor, in 1876, most of my Negro friends voted for Hampton.

What have I been doing since I grew up? Well, I have been busy trying to make a living. I worked for various white folks in this community and sometime for the railroads here, in a minor capacity. My younger years were spent in the quest of an education. For the past thirty years I have been the porter for the *State* paper company, Columbia's morning newspaper. As I became proficient in the work, the Gonzales boys grew fond of me. While the youngest one, Honorable William E. Gonzales, was absent in the diplomatic service in Cuba and in Peru for eight years for President Wilson, looked after the needs of Mr. Ambrose Gonzales. Shortly before he died, Honorable William E. Gonzales returned. He has since been editor and publisher of the *State*, as well as principal owner.

You ask, if I have applied for an old age pension. No, I have not. I am old enough to qualify, I guess, but I understand, you cannot get a pension if you have a job. If that is so, I shall never enjoy any pension money. I would not leave serving my friend, Captain William E. Gonzales, for any pension that might be offered me.

Note from the original interviewer: "This man is well-educated, speaks no dialect. He received his education from Northern teachers in freedman aid, equal to the modern high school curriculum. He afterward studied in Boston. He reads, writes and speaks excellent English."[17]

SLAVE STORIES OF JERRY HILL

Living with his married daughter is an old Negro slave by the name of Jerry Hill. He was born January 12, 1852. He and his mother were owned by Jim Fernandes who had a plantation between Union and Jonesville, South Carolina. His father was a slave owned by another white man on an adjoining plantation. "Uncle" Jerry was nine years old when the war began, and thirteen when he was set free. He was born near Rocky Creek, which ran into Fairforest Creek. He was always treated kindly by his master. He was taught to plow and work on the farm, which he did regularly; though he always took his time and would not let anybody hurry him. He said that he had always taken his time to do his farm work, so got along fine with all for whom he worked. He says that he always had plenty to eat; yet most of the Negroes had to eat ash bread. This is cornbread which is cooked in hot ashes raked from the fireplace. Once a week he was given biscuits, though this was a luxury to colored folks. He said, that when a slave had to have a whipping, he was taken to a whipping post in Jonesville. A bullwhip was used for the punishment and it brought the blood from the bare back of the man or woman being whipped. One day a grown slave was given 150 lashes with the bullwhip, for teaching the young boys to gamble. He saw this punishment administered. He had climbed a tree where he could get a better view. He said that several slaves were being whipped that day for various things, and there were several men standing around watching the whipping. He said that he was laughing at the victim, when some bystander looked up and saw him; "That boy needs 150 lashes, too," he said. "He is laughing at the punishment being given." So his master told the bystander to get the boy and give him the lashing if he thought he needed it. When he was led up to the whipping post, some man there shook his head at the bystander; so the boy did not get whipped. Jerry says that the sister of Jim Fernandas used to carry a bullwhip around her neck when she walked out on the farm, and would apply it herself to any slave she thought needed it.

"When the Yankee soldiers came," he said, "my master had to hide out for a while, as he had gotten into some trouble with them at Union. They would search the house occasionally and then go into the woods looking for him. One day the soldiers caught him down on the branch and killed him. As the Yankee soldiers would come to the plantation, they would leave their worn-out horses and take our good ones. They also stole meat, hams, sugar etc.; but they were pretty quiet most of the time. One of our neighbors caught a Yankee stealing his horse and killed him right there. His name was Bill Isom. All his family is now dead. The soldiers would slip around and steal a good horse and ride it off. We would never see that horse again. After we were told by my master that we were now free and could go to work wherever we chose, my mother hired me out to a man and I stayed with him two years. It was pretty hard to make a living after we were free, but I worked hard and always got on."[18]

ISAIAH MOORE'S STORIES

Isaiah Moore was, by surviving accounts, one of the great storytellers of the slavery era in South Carolina. The following accounts from the Works Progress Administration's Slave Narrative Project are what survive of his tales. His versions of the biblical tales of Nicodemus and Adam and Eve are examples of how Black preachers and storytellers of that day, who were forced into illiteracy, would add their imaginations and hearsay to make such stories vivid to their listeners.

Interestingly, the version of Nicodemus's story told here is similar to one that was recorded by the white folklorist Roark Bradford from an unlettered Black Tennessee minister named John Wesley Henning, who was also known as "Preacher Wes," for Bradford's 1928 volume Ol' Man Adam and His Chillun. *This book would inspire the 1936 musical motion picture* The Green Pastures, *which was one of the first major productions that portrayed Black folklore and, as with Moore's and Henning's stories, described the major biblical figures as Black.*

Interview with George McAlilley, Eighty-Four Years Old

George McAlilley lives with his son-in-law, daughter and small grandchildren in a one-room frame house, with a lean-to shed room annex. The annex has no fireplace, no window, is ten feet by eight feet in dimension and it is in this pen that George and the two small children sleep. The house is three miles north of the town of Winnsboro, set back in a cotton field, five hundred yards east of U.S. 21.

George gathers the firewood from the neighboring woods, picks blackberries in summer and assists in the harvesting of cotton from the fields in September.

"'Bout the tale you want to hear. Well, Preacher Alfred Moore, a colored slave, search de scripture for names for his children. One boy him name Isaiah and one name Phillip. They both was mighty good slaves of Dr. Walter Brice, our doctor. My master and Dr. Price's son, Marse Thomas, marry sisters and I see a heap of Isaiah and Phillip. Isaiah had a tale about Niggerdemos [Nicodemus] and Phil had a tale about a eunuch. Which one you want to hear? Both? I'm getting tired. I'll just tell Isaiah's tale 'bout Niggerdemos. You has seen de blisters on sycamore trees? I knows you have. Well, Isaiah allow they come 'bout in this way: In the days of the disciples there was a small colored man named Niggerdemos that was a Republican and run an eating house in Jerusalem.

"He done his own cooking and serving at de tables. He heard the tramp, tramp, tramp of the multitude a coming, and he asked: 'What that going on outside?' They told him the disciples done borrowed a colt and was having a parade over de city. Niggerdemos thought de good Lord would cure him of the lumbago in his back. Hearing folks a shouting, he threw down his dish rag, jerked off his apron, and run for to see all that was going on, but having short legs he couldn't see nothing. A big sycamore tree stood in de line of the parade, so Niggerdemos climbed up it, going high enough for to see all. The Savior tell him: 'Come down; we going to eat at your house, Niggerdemos.' Niggerdemos come down so fast, when he hear that, he scrape the bark off the tree in many places. Niggerdemos was sure cured of the lumbago but sycamores been blistered ever since. Next time you pass a sycamore tree, look how it is blistered.

"Isaiah is asleep now, in the white folks graveyard at Concord Church. I has seen his tombstone. On it is wrote his age and day of his death. Below that, is just this: 'As good as ever fluttered.' His young Master Tommie put it there."[19]

INTERVIEW WITH CHARITY MOORE, SEVENTY-FIVE YEARS OLD

One quarter of a mile north of Woodward station and one hundred yards east of U.S. 21, is the beautiful residence of Mr. T.W. Brice. In the backyard is a two-room frame house. In this house lives Charity Moore and another aged Negro woman, said to be an octogenarian. They occupy the house together and exist on the goodness and charity of Mr. Brice. Charity was born a slave of Mr. Brice's father, and has lived all her days in his immediate family.

"Don't you remember my pa, Isaiah Moore? Course you does! He was the Uncle Remus of all the White children around dese parts. He sure was! I seen him setting with you, Marse Johnnie, Marse Boyce, and Dickie Brice, in the backyard many a time. You all was asking him questions about the tale he was a telling and him shaking his sides a laughing. He told all them tales 'bout the fox and the rabbit, the squirrel, brer moccasin, and such, long before they come out in a book. He sure did!

"My ma name Nancy, that was pa's wedded wife. There was no bigamous nor concubine business going on with us. My brothers was Dave, Solomon, Fortune, Charlie, and Brice. My sisters was Haley, Fannie, Sarah, Frances, Mary, and Margaret. Hold your writin' dere a minute. There was thirteen. Oh, yes, I left out Teeta. That rounds them up, a baker's dozen.

"White folks, my pa had Bible tales he never told the white children. Did you know that my pa knew the catechism from cover to cover, and from the back end to the starting end? Concord Church gave him a Bible for answering every question in the catechism. Here it is. [Producing catechism published and dated 1840.] My pa maybe never told you any Bible tales he told the colored children. He allowed that the first man, Adam, was a Black man. Eve was ginger cake color, with long black hair down to her ankles. That Adam had just one worriment in the garden and that was his kinky hair. Eve hate to see him sad, because she loved her husband as all wives ought to do, if they don't.

"Well, Adam played with Eve's hair; run his fingers through it and sigh. Eve couldn't do that with his kinky hair. The devil set up in de plum bushes and took notice of the trouble going on. Every day Eve's hair grew longer and longer. Adam get sadder and sadder. The devil in the plum bushes get gladder and gladder. There come a day that Adam excused himself from promenading in among the flower beds with his arms around Eve, a holding up her hair. The devil took the shape of a serpent, glided after Eve, and stole up and twisted himself up into that hair far enough to whisper in one of them pretty ears: 'Somebody's got something for to tell you that will make Adam glad and like himself again! Keep your ears open all day long.' Then the serpent untangled himself, dropped to the ground, and skeedaddled to the red apple tree, close by the fountain. He knew that Eve was going there to bathe. He beat her there, because she was walking sort of slow, grieving about Adam and thinking about how to cheer him up. When she got there, the old devil done changed from a snake to a angel of light, a male angel, I reckon. He took off his silk beaver hat, flourished his gold headed cane, and allowed: 'Good morning! Lovely day! What a beautiful apple, just in your reach too, ahem!' Eve say: 'I'm not been introduced,' 'Well,' said the devil, 'My subjects call me Prince, because I'm the Prince of light. My given name is Lucifer. I's at your service, dear lady.' Eve reflected: 'A prince, he'll be a king some day.'

"Then the devil say: 'Of course, one of your beauty will one day be a queen. I seen a sadness on your lovely face as you come along. What might be your worry?' Eve told him and he allowed: 'Just get Adam to eat one bite out that apple above your head and in a night his hair will grow as long, be as black, and as straight as yours. She alllowed: "We ain't allowed to eat of the fruit of the tree in the midst of the garden. We dare not touch it, lest we die.' Then Satan stepped a distance this way, then another way and come back and say: 'Gracious lady! This tree is not in the midst of de garden. The one in the midst is that crabapple tree over yonder. Of course de good Lord didn't want you to eat crabapples.'

"The devil done got her all mixed up. The apple looked so good, she reached up, and quick as you can say 'Jack Robinson,' she bite the apple and run to Adam with de rest of it and say: 'Husband eat quick and your hair will be as long, as black, and straight as mine, in the morning.' While he was eating it, and taking the last swallow of the apple, he was reminded of the disobedience, and choked twice. Ever since then, a man have an 'Adam's Apple' to 'mind him of de sin of disobedience.

"It wasn't long before the Lord come a looking for them. Adam got so scared his face turned white, right then, and next morning, he was a white man with long hair but worse off than when he was colored. There was more to that tale but I don't remember it now.[20]

A SON OF SLAVES CLIMBS UP

The Reverend John B. Elliott, ABA, AM, DD, 1315 Liberty Hill Avenue, Columbia, South Carolina, is the son of slaves.

He was born at Mount Olive, North Carolina, in 1869, and missed being a slave by only four years. His college degrees were won at Shaw University, Raleigh, North Carolina, and the degree of doctor of divinity was conferred on him by Allen University of Columbia, South Carolina.

Sitting on the parsonage piazza recently, the Rector of St. Anna's Episcopal Church talked about his struggle for education, and his labors up from slavery.

"I was born at Mount Olive, Noth Carolina, the son of Soloman Elliott and Alice (Roberts) Elliott. They were slaves when they married, and I escaped bondage by only four years, since slaves were not freed in the South, until 1865.

"My father was owned by Robert W. Williams, of Mount Olive, and he was the most highly prized Negro in the vicinity. He was a natural carpenter and builder. Often he would go to the woods and pick out trees for the job in hand. Some of the houses he built there are standing today. Mother was equally trained and well equipped to make a home and keep it neat and clean. When they were free in 1865, half the community was eager to employ them and pay them well for their services. And, when I came along, they were living in their own house and prospering.

"I chose a religious career when quite a boy, and, when I was ready for college, I was much pleased. I finished at Shaw University at Raleigh, took a year's study at Columbia University in New York and then finished a religious course at the Bishop Payne Divinity School at Petersburg, Virginia, where most of the colored clergymen of the Episcopal Church are finished. After I felt that I was fairly well fitted to begin my clerical work, I chose South Carolina as my field.

"My first assignment was at Waccamaw Neck, a little below Georgetown, South Carolina, and a big industrial center.

"There the Negro population is keen for wine and whiskey. One of the men whom I was interested in, was pretty tipsy when I called, and, as I sat and talked with him, he said: 'You're drunk, too.' This surprised me, and I asked him why he thought so. 'Well, you got your vest and collar on backwards, so you must be drunk!'

"Since, I have had pastorates at Aiken, Peak, Rock Hill and Walterboro. From Walterboro I came to Columbia as pastor of St. Anna's Episcopal Church and the missions of Ann's at New Brookland and St. Thomas at Eastover. I presume I have done pretty well in this field, since the Right Reverend Bishop Kirkman G. Finlay, DD, appointed me arch-deacon for Negro work in upper South Carolina.

"As I was coming away from the bishop's office, I was accompanied by another colored rector, who had very short legs. I am six feet, four inches in height, and he looked up at me as we walked along and asked quizzically: 'How long should a man's legs be?' I smiled and told him I thought, perhaps, every man should have legs long enough to reach to the ground. Yes, of course, we laughed at each other, but my argument won, because Bishop Finlay is about six feet, three inches, and I told my short friend: 'When Bishop Finlay and I talk, we are able to look each other in the eye on the level.'

"I married Susan McMahan, a colored schoolteacher, and the Lord has blessed us with a son, John B. Jr., a fine woodworker, like his grandfather was, and two sweet daughters. Alice, the older one, is a teacher in the public schools of Columbia and Annie is a student. Our home life has always been pleasant and unusually sunny.

"I had one very humorous experience three years ago when I was invited to deliver an address near Mount Olive, North Carolina, to a convention of young people. Arriving about ten o'clock that day, I was met by a citizen who told me he was assigned to introduce me that evening. As we rode along, I cautioned him not to boost me too highly. He said little.

"When the big, and, I may say, expectant audience was seated that night, he arose and seemed much embarrassed, ultimately saying: 'Ladies and gentlemen, I have an unpleasant duty to perform this evening.'

Then, pointing at me, he went on: 'I don't know this man, much. Fact is, I only know two things about him. One is, he has never been in jail; and the other is, I never could figure why.'

"No, I am not related to the late Robert Bruce Elliott by ties of consanguinity. He was successively twice a member of Congress from South Carolina, and a member and speaker of the South Carolina House of Representatives in 1876. Perhaps these honors came to him because he had a good education before he met the opportunity for service.

"When I think of the '60s–'70s period, I am surprised that recent slaves, suddenly placed in administrative positions of honor and trust, did as well as they did.

"In the seventy-two years since slavery, I have noted much improvement along the road, and I am sure that our nation has far less discord now, than it had when I was a small lad. And, when one can note progress in our march toward the light, I guess that ought to be sufficient for my optimism."[21]

THE SLAVE STORY OF LEWIS EVANS

The Spartanburg Herald *newspaper of November 12, 1933, included this anecdote from a story titled "Former Slave Tells Story of Days Before 'De (Civil) War,'" regarding an elderly Black resident of Spartanburg named Lewis Evans's recollections of slavery. It shows how during slavery, African Americans often concealed their true feelings from their owners.*

I was at my old master's Squire Evans when the war broke out, but Master Evans died just before the war. That same fall, eighty-three of us were sold on the block on the old stage road in Laurens County running from Greenville to Newberry. One morning I was sent to Mr. Lewis Power's blacksmith shop to get the paper telling about the war. I come back home and goes in the front of the house and called my mistress and said, "Here's the paper, Miss."

She took the paper and began to read it. After a while, she took up her apron and began to wipe the tears from her eyes and then I gets to crying. My mistress said, "Well the war is started and I've got two brothers in the army and they may be killed."

Old lady Winnie was sweeping the floor right then. I can remember it like it was yesterday. Old Lady Winnie, she says, "Old Abe Lincoln, the black-headed rascal ought to have his head shot off." After that, Old Winnie goes down to a Negro named Aunt Dock, and I follows her and I hear her say, "God bless old Abe Lincoln—we gonna be free!" Then she and old Aunt Dock jump up and down and shout like fools. And she had just said in the kitchen before the mistress that Abe Lincoln's head should be shot off. I was young and didn't know what this was all about, or why old lady Winnie would say one thing for my mistress and another thing to Old Aunt Dock, so I keeps following her and Old Winnie and Old Aunt Dock goes from place to place and keep telling them Negroes that Old Abe Lincoln had freed us, and then they would start to shouting. She said one thing for my mistress and something else to the Negroes."[22]

A RECONSTRUCTION LEADER'S DAUGHTER

The following is a 1938 interview with the daughter of Bishop Richard Harvey Cain. Bishop Cain was a Reconstruction hero, congressman and the founding pastor of Charleston's Mother Emanuel AME Church.

1938—ANN J. EDWARDS, eighty-one, Fort Worth, Texas, was born a slave of John Cook, of Arlington County, Virginia. He manumitted his slaves in 1857. Four years later, Ann was adopted by Richard H. Cain, a colored preacher. He was elected to the Forty-Fifth Congress in 1876, and remained in Washington, D.C., until his death in 1887. Ann married James E. Edwards, graduate of Howard College, a preacher. She now lives with her granddaughter, Mary Foster, at 804 East Fourth Street, Fort Worth, Texas.

"I shall gladly relate the story of my life. I was born a slave on January 27th, 1856, and my master's name was John J. Cook, who was a resident of Arlington County, Virginia. He moved to Washington, D.C., when I was nearly two years old and immediately gave my parents their freedom. They separated within a year after that, and my mother earned our living, working as a hairdresser until her death in 1861. I was then adopted by Richard H. Cain, a minister of the Gospel in the African Methodist Church.

"I remember the beginning of the war well. The conditions made a deep impression on my mind, and the atmosphere of Washington was charged with excitement and expectations. There existed considerable need for assistance to the Negroes who had escaped after the war began, and Reverend Cain took a leading part in rendering aid to them. They came into the city without clothes or money and no idea of how to secure employment. A large number were placed on farms, some given employment as domestics and still others mustered into the federal army.

"The city was one procession of men in blue and the air was full of martial music. The fife and drum could be heard almost all the time, so you may imagine what emotions a colored person of my age would experience, especially as father's church was a center for congregating the Negroes and advising them. That was a difficult task, because a large majority were illiterate and ignorant.

"The year father was called to Charleston, South Carolina, to take charge of a church, we became the center of considerable trouble. It was right after the close of the war. In addition to his ministerial duties, father managed a newspaper and became interested in politics. He was elected a delegate to the Constitutional Convention of South Carolina in 1868. He was also elected a Republican member of the state senate and served from 1868 to 1872. Then he became the Republican candidate for the United States Representative of the Charleston district, was elected and served in the 45th Congress from March 4, 1877, to March 3, 1879.

"You can imagine the bitter conflict his candidacy brought on. A Negro running for public office against a white person in a Southern state that was strong for slavery does not seem the sensible thing for a man to do, but he did and was, of course, successful. From the moment he became delegate to the Constitutional Convention a guard was necessary night and day to watch our home. He was compelled to have a bodyguard wherever he went. We, his family, lived in constant fear at all times. Many times mother pleaded with him to cease his activities, but her pleadings were of no avail.

"In the beginning the resentment was not so pronounced. The white people were shocked and dejected over the outcome of the war, but gradually recovered. As they did, determination to establish order and prosperity developed, and they resented the Negro taking part in public affairs. On the other side of the cause was the excess and obstinate actions of some ignorant

Negroes, acting under ill advice. Father was trying to prevent excesses being done by either side. He realized that the slaves were unfit, at that time, to take their place as dependable citizens, for the want of experience and wisdom, and that there would have to be mental development and wisdom learned by his race, and that such would only come by a gradual process.

"He entered the contest in the interest of his own race, primarily, but as a whole, to do justice to all. No one could change his course. He often stated, 'It is by the divine will that I am in this battle.'

"The climax of the resentment against him took place when he was chosen Republican candidate to the House of Representatives. He had to maintain an armed guard at all times. Several times, despite these guards, attempts were made to either burn the house or injure some member of the family. If it had not been for the fact that the officials of the city and county were afraid of the federal government, which gave aid in protecting him, the mob would have succeeded in harming him.

"A day or two before election a mob gathered suddenly in front of the house, and we all thought the end had come. Father sent us all upstairs, and said he would, if necessary, give himself up to the mob and let them satisfy their vengeance on him, to save the rest of us.

"While he was talking, mother noticed another body of men in the alley. They were certainly sinister looking. Father told us to prepare for the worst, saying, 'What they plan to do is for those in front to engage the attention of ourselves and the guard, then those in the rear will fire the place and force us out.' He was calm throughout it all, but mother was greatly agitated and I was crying.

"The chief of the guard called father for a parley. The mob leader demanded that father come out for a talk. Then the sheriff and deputies appeared and he addressed the crowd of men, and told them if harm came to us the city would be placed under martial law. The men then dispersed, after some discussion among themselves.

"Father moved to Washington, took the oath of office and served until March 4, 1879. He then received the appointment of bishop of the African Methodist Church and served until his death in Washington, on January 18, 1887.

"I began my schooling in Charleston and continued in Washington, where I entered Howard College, but did not continue until graduation. I met James E. Edwards, another student, who graduated in 1881, and my heart overruled my desire for an education. We married and he entered the ministry and was called to Dallas, Texas. He remained two years, then we were called to Los Angeles. The Negroes there were privileged to enter public eating establishments, but an owner we patronized told us the following: 'After a time, I was compelled to refuse service to Negroes because they abused the privilege. They came in in a boisterous manner and crowded and shoved other patrons. It was due to a lack of wisdom and education.'

"That was true. The white people tried to give the Negro his rights and he abused the privilege because he was ignorant, a condition he could not then help.

"My husband and I were called to Kansas City in 1896 and from there to many other towns. Finally we came to Waco, and he had charge of a church there when he died, in 1927. We had a pleasant married life and I tried to do my duty as a pastor's wife and help elevate my race. We were blessed with three children, and the only one now living is in Boston, Massachusetts.

"I now reside with my granddaughter, Mary Foster, and this shack is the best her husband can afford. In fact, we are living in destitute circumstances. It is depressing to me, after having lived a life in a comfortable home. It is the Lord's will and I must accept what is provided. There is a purpose for all things. I shall soon go to meet my Maker, with the satisfaction of having done my duty—first, to my race, second, to mankind."

—Ann J. Edwards[23]

WASHINGTON'S SICK HORSE: CURED BY NEGRO FAITH DOCTOR

The following tale is a good example of how storytelling was passed down through the generations in a vivid manner, as the speaker assumed the role of his great-grandfather in telling the story.

Hampton Fielder, Negro janitor, aged sixty-five, living at 1715 Gadsden Street, Columbia, South Carolina, is the great-grandson of a slave who, according to slave tradition, cured the sick horse of President George Washington during his visit to Columbia, May 22 to May 24, 1791. The president duly records being delayed in his schedule by a day, "because one of his horses had the bots." He makes no mention of treatments in his diary.

Fielder says his great-grandfather, then a slave of the Fielders, married Eliza Hampton, a daughter of the young slave doctor, who treated animals and people by faith, from 1789 to 1825. At that time, General Wade Hampton had three thousand slaves. Fielder said with apparent pride:

"My grand mammy was the best looking girl on the Hampton plantations. She told me much about the visit of the great George Washington and his reception here, as told by her daddy.

"My mammy, as I always called grand mammy, say her daddy told her, 'The slaves hereabouts was as proud of General Washington as the White folks were, when he came here to see us. Lord have mercy child, we had big times form the highest buckra [White person], like Governor Charles Pinckney, General Wade Hampton, Commodore [Alexander] Gillon, and the White folks like that, to the littlest slave pickaninny. The slaves was sure thrilled, because they heard that General Washington was going to free his slaves right soon. Yes sir, he done made up his mind to that effect.

"I see the joy of the faces of the buckras, as they set out in their fine carriages, with their prancing horses, to meet and welcome the great man. The whole town was parading all along State Street in front of the state house when the party got there. Governor Charles Pinckney and his staff, and many more, stood at attention.

"When General Washington was seen, Governor Pinckney ran down from the steps of the state house, as pert as a little boy, and grabbed both of General Washington's hands and told him how honored he was to see him in South Carolina. General Washington smiled and said the pleasure was all his own. Then the general turned around and faced everybody in the street saying, 'I'm happy to see the new capital of South Carolina. By laying it out in the woods, you have a chance to make it what it ought to be.' Child, how the crowd did cheer and laugh.

"Then Governor Pinckney and many of the biggest buckras get in their carriages and go with the general to Governor Pinckney's home, not far from the Congaree River and in sight of Granby, where the general was at home while he was in Columbia. There was more doings while the great man was here, but I didn't see all of them. The slaves heard that one of the general horses was sick with the bots [bot flies] and general and was distressed about it. The horse doctor come to the Pinckney stables and forced down powders, but the horse appeared to get sicker.

"One slave come after me and told me about it. We decided to go to the stables and saw what we can do, when no buckra was looking. When we got there, the horse was laying down just like he did when he has the bots. His eyes was reddish and his hair stood out from the skin. The hay in the rack and the corn in the trough not even tasted. That was about eleven o'clock. I step in the stall and the poor sick horse look at me so pleading. I can do nothing by myself, so I ask God to help me.

"As I lay my hands on stroke the poor horse from the root of the tail to its nose, I prayed, 'The same yesterday, today, and forever.' I done this three times. Then as I get up, I stand and uttered three times, 'In the name of the Father, the Son, and The Holy Ghost. Amen.' And bless the Lord, I looked out and there stood General Washington and General Hampton with their hats off, not saying a word. Us slaves went away, and soon the buckras go back to the house.

"About twelve o'clock, we go back to the stable and sure as you're living, the sick horse got up, shook himself, and drink from as tub. Then he walked over and took a bite of hay from the rack. He saw the corn in the trough and start to eat, just like he was hungry. We get over behind the barn, and pretty soon General Washington and General Hampton came back smiling. And the great Washington said, 'Well Hampton, now that my horse is able, I must start on my journey by daylight tomorrow.'"[24]

3
Tales of the Supernatural

These stories, collected mostly in the 1930s, reflect the role of the supernatural in the daily life of many Black South Carolinians. Many educated Black people once dismissed such tales as an embarrassing hindrance against their progress toward mainstream assimilation, but today, many understand these stories as a historical aspect of African American folk culture.

CONJURING

Some colored people have a way of conjuring a person whom they do not like, by taking an opportunity when that person is in his or her house, and before that visitor leaves, of spilling a little salt at the front door. When the visitor leaves, he or she will have to step over on the salt and thus be conjured. This will cause the person to have pains like that of rheumatism, or in some way be afflicted physically.

When one colored fellow is in love with a girl, and yet another of the same race seems to have the upper hand with the girl, he will adopt some plan to conjure the rival for the girl's affections. He may make some brew, or "doctor" some candy, anything to cause the rival to eat what he wants him to eat. Pretty soon, the rival will be eliminated by death, disease, sickness, or something which will incapacitate him from pressing his suit for the girl in question. This is not considered murder, but is termed "conjuring" a rival.

—George Brown[25]

GHOST STORIES

I was living at 123 Bull Street when I was terribly frightened by something nearly took all of my nerves away. The people with whom I lived told me not to go out and stay out late at night; but I thought they were selfish and jealous, and I did not pay any attention to what they said. Night after night, I went out and stayed until twelve o'clock. Then one night came when my going was stopped without having to be told,

The house in which I lived is next to Avery Institute with a yard of beautiful shrubbery which makes it very haunted-looking at night. Very seldom are people seen passing in that somewhat secluded section of Charleston at night.

Night after night, I would be the only one walking along when, on an eventful night just as I turned to go into the side entrance to my room in the rear, in the tree under which I had to walk I saw a cat, which did not frighten me until it turned to a calf of about two years old. My hair stood straight on my head and I became so weak that my voice was just above a whisper. Swabs of perspiration fell from me. When I had recovered from the shock, I ran and the animal must have followed me; I could hear it galloping behind me as I ran home a few rods from the scene. Looking back as I almost burst down the door, the peculiar thing was no longer visible.

—Mrs. S.C. Ladson[26]

In rural districts, the people usually say that after six o'clock in the evening ghosts leave graveyards to go walking during the night. Some are said to be good and some bad. Two are usually together, a good one and a bad one. When one is frightened by a ghost, one is believed to have strayed from the good manner of living.

It was about seven-thirty one winter night in the country, when a friend and I were going to visit another. We had to cross a ditch, which led to a long line of thickly clustered bushes and vines. When we were approaching this thicket, and about five feet from its entrance used by pedestrians, there appeared in the center of the path a man about nine feet tall and whose feet were about a foot from the ground. This man had no face, but stood erect like a soldier. We grabbed each other and began to run and scream when all of a sudden a strong wind came and blew us to the ground before we could raise our voices high enough to be heard. It was about ten o'clock when we were discovered by a group of people passing while our nerves were still shattered. This was not far from a graveyard. When we told of the tall man we saw, an old lady told us that that man with his feet above the ground was said to be the tallest man in the world when he was alive, and that he guarded that place for it was there that he had lost a girl be had loved.

People deny the existence of ghosts, but I do not. Once I thought it was all folly and ideas as a result of superstition and ignorance; but I believe in ghosts because I can see them.

—Joe C. Williams[27]

PLAT EYES

Plat eyes come into being when one buries a treasure and places the head of a murdered man in the hole with the valuables. If an intruder approaches the spot, the plat eye will arise out of the ground in the guise of a six-legged calf or headless hog and frighten the trespasser away.

This creature has nothing to do with a ghost. It has its being entirely apart from life of any kind. There are, it seems, in the sea island regions, some animal ghosts, but the plat eye comes into existence when someone slays a man, cuts off his head and places the head in a hole with a treasure which is to be hidden for a time. The slaying of a man and the burying of his head brings about the birth of a spirit which has the power to change its form at will, when an intruder comes too near to the treasure.

George Brown says that sometimes the plat eye is a big black hog with enormous white tusks; other times it may be a five-legged calf or hunched-back yellow dog with two tails. If anyone save the owner of the treasure approaches the tree where the money or other valuables are buried, the plat eye will do its best to divert the person's attention from the spot by running around in a circle, or jumping violently up and down, or acting otherwise like a beast possessed by seven devils.

—George Brown[28]

THOMAS GOODWATER'S GHOST STORY

I always play with ghosts because I was born with a "call." I can see the ghost just as plain as ever. Sometime I see some I know and again others I don't know. Only thing you can't see their feet because they walk off the ground. When I use to see them, my sister would put sand on the fire then they would go and I wouldn't see any for a long time. One morning, my uncle was passing a church and a ghost appeared on the porch. My uncle had a dog with him. He start to run and the dog start to run, too, and down the road they went. He didn't have on anything but his shirt and he say he run so fast 'til the wind had his shirt-tail stiff as a board. He couldn't outrun the dog, nor could the dog out run him.

—Thomas Goodwater[29]

HAG STORIES

Hags are not spirits of the dead, but spirits of mean, jealous living people. A hag rarely rides a mule, but will ride a good horse all but to death. Next morning the beast will be lame, lathered with sweat, its mane and tail plaited and tied into knots that can hardly be loosened. Hags also ride people asleep and cause horrible dreams as they sit on the chest of those they smother or choke. They swallow voices so the victim cannot be heard in calling for help. No door can keep hags out, but they are curious and suspicious, and will pass nothing without giving it close examination. They will stop to count and measure every straw in a broom, every hole in a sieve hung beside a stable or house door, before they go inside. By the time they finish the morning star may shine, and halt their wicked work, for they dare not be seen in daylight. Some hags are experienced and can count very fast, but a loaded gun laid across the head of the bed will keep most hags away, for they all fear the smell of gunpowder.

—Mildred Hare[30]

At night after you go to bed, the old hag comes in the house and peeps on you, gets on you, and rides you. Nearly rides you to death. Looks like a skeleton—nothing but bones. They fall on you, ride you, and worry you to death. They tell you their name sometimes.

—Dromgoole Ham[31]

FOUR MEN AND THE TREASURE

One night a spirit appeared to four men at the same time. The spirit told the four men of a vault that contained all the wealth of a family who were killed in one of America's first wars. The men met together and discussed the plans in detail.

The treasure would make them all wealthy, the men and their children and their children's children. The men knew that the spirit of a dead man guarded the treasure. It was said that in olden times a slave would promise to look after his master's treasure. So, when a hole was dug and the treasure was ready to be hidden, the slave was beheaded. His head was thrown into the hole first, then the pot of treasure, and the body of the slave on top. A tree would be planted to mark the spot. Sometimes, for years and years, the treasure would lie unmolested, protected by the spirit of the faithful slave. But again, the guardian would tire of his task and would assume the form of a living person. It would appear in a dream to someone it loved and tell where the treasure could be found. This is the way the four men found out about the treasure. The spirit told them of many trials they would have before they could get the treasure, but they knew it would be theirs if they could endure. Without whole-hearted Christian faith they knew that a person seldom could hold out to the end.

The four men agreed to follow the instructions given them by the spirit. They took a Bible and a hymn book to the place—along with a watch so they might know when to sing and when to pray. The tools for digging were placed in their right positions. The men faced a certain direction, singing and praying at intervals, unconscious of the world around and the roaring wind, the moaning and groaning of monster beasts, rattling of chains, voices asking questions to which no answer dared be given. At a certain time the signal for digging was given when the singing of hymns and the reading of the Bible were done as the spirit said. Throughout the whole ceremony, not a word should be uttered except the words in the hymns and Bible. The men dug, dug, and dug every night for almost two weeks.

At last they reached a large pot. The men had to build platforms on which to rest the pot as it was raised to the top. Now, three of the men were very strong and healthy, but the fourth was weakly. He was always behind the rest. The others nagged him constantly as they went to and from the place where they were digging. He became very exhausted and thought once or twice he would give up. But he kept on until the night they found the pot. When the pot with the contents, which were to make the men's children's children wealthy, was about five feet from the surface, one of them said to the little man, "Pull your end with your weak self."

In an instant, the element became black and a wind, emerged from out of nowhere, turned the earth into a turmoil. The thunder roared and the lightning flashed uncontrollably. Down, down went the pot with all its wealth. The three strong men fell into the hole with the pot. All except the one who could not keep up were buried. The little man was knocked unconscious for several minutes, but he did not fall in. When he came to and did not see any of his companions, he knew what had happened. He began to dig and, when he had dug for about four feet, uncovered one of the men who was trying to push his way to the top. The two dug until the third was reached, and he, in turn, helped dig for the fourth. The three dug, dug and dug until they feared the other had gone down with the pot. But they decided to dig a few feet more before giving up.

Reaching the depth at which the pot had been buried they found the fourth man—barely breathing. The fourth man was the one who had spoken words not out of the Bible nor the hymnbook. Sometime later, when they had gotten over the shock, they began digging for the pot again but were told by the spirit that their digging was in vain. They had not followed instructions, and they died as poor as they always had been.[32]

When a person dies, according to a Negro preacher, his spirit does not go immediately to heaven nor hell. In fact, it has a long wait for it can have no permanent place of habitation until after judgment day. However, the good get part of their reward immediately for as their bodies lie beneath the sod, so their spirits find rest and peace until the great day, but not so with the wicked.

Restless spirits are called "haants" that come back to harass the living. They cannot rest; they wander on the face of the earth—tormented as a result of their fate. But not "'till Gabriel blow 'e horn," said an old minister, "will they actually be thrown into the blaze of hell." Brimstone and fire is said to be the reward for the wicked forever. Nor until then will the good have their reward. They will go to an actual heaven that the Bible describes—a place of golden streets, white robes, wings, and milk with honey.

—Laura L. Middleton[33]

4

Animal and Trickster Tales

As Dr. Ousmane Sene mentioned in the first chapter of this book, one of the African traditions that has survived among the Black American population is the use of animal stories to teach life lessons to all. While this tradition has evaporated in recent years, volumes such as Folklore of the Sea Islands *(1923),* South Carolina Folk Tales *(1941) and* Afro-American Folk Lore *(1892) collected these tales. The folklorists originally wrote these stories in their informants' dialect, which makes them difficult for the modern reader to comprehend. I have modified the dialect for the contemporary reader while retaining some elements of the speech patterns of the speaker to make the stories easier for present and future generations to understand.*

A STORYTELLER AND HIS STORY

This selection is from the first collection of South Carolina's Black folk tales, Afro-American Folk Lore Told Round Cabin Fires on the Sea Islands of South Carolina, *by Abbie M.H. Christensen. A White woman of Massachusetts, she arrived on the Sea Islands near Beaufort, South Carolina in 1864, where she says she met a Black storyteller named Prince Baskin in the following manner and collected his tales in her 1892 volume.*

His name, so he tells me, is "Prince"; his title, "Baskin"; age, "'bout sixty or seventy, I 'spec's, Missus." Small and short of stature, very dark skinned, but not ugly enough to be interesting. Prince Baskin looks commonplace enough to a casual observer. But to see him once in animated conversation would delight any lover of the comical and send a true disciple of Darwin into ecstasies. No one can deny that he looks much less of a man than a monkey, with his absurd gestures, and all the frantic jerks and bobs and dives to right and left, that render still more comical the short figure set off by a bobtailed coat of faded army blue. In his own words, he "been born and raised on the Nat Heywood place, a nice plantation on de Cumbee."

He regards the rabbit stories with much respect, evidently considering them types of human experience in general and his own in particular. He considers all the strategy of the rabbit quite admirable so long as it is successful, even though it should involve the cruelest treachery. (Indeed, I fear the sentiment is general.)

"But I was going to tell you about my old granddaddy. I often heard him tell how he was bring over from Africa in a ship when 'e was a boy. The white man left the ship behind and gone ashore in a small boat; an' when they meet up with my granddaddy and a whole parcel more, young boys like, all from de same village, they hired them with piece of red flannel and things to go along with them. But when they get them on board the ship, they bring them over to this country an' sell them for slaves. They bring my granddaddy to Charleston and Ol' Master Heywood buy him. When I was a small boy, he been very old. Too old for work, and I use to have it for my task to mind him. So he tell me a heap of these stories, if I only could remember them, that he use to hear way over in Africa.

"One time old Brer Wolf was growing a field of corn when one morning, he saw some rabbit tracks in the cornfield and some half-eaten corncobs all over the place. The wolf said, 'Lord have mercy, that rabbit been here to teef [steal] my corn.' So the wolf built himself a scarecrow to scare Brer Rabbit away. The next night, the rabbit came to the cornfield and said, 'That wolf must think I is a fool to be scared by that thing,' and ate up more of the wolf's corn that night.

"So the wolf got up the next morning, yawned and stretched," Ernest dramatized the yawning and stretching for comic effect. "He looked around the field and said, 'That rabbit done eat up my corn again. I'll fix that teef [thief].' So he got a lump of tar, put a hat on its head, a carrot for its nose, buttons for its eyes, and an old coat to wear. He called this thing a tar baby, and when his wife asked him what he was doing, he said, 'Honey, we gonna have some rabbit stew tonight.'

"Right that night, the rabbit looked around the wolf's cornfield and saw the tar baby. Since it was dark, he couldn't see what the tar baby really was, so he walked up to the tar baby, shook his hand, and said, 'Howdy stranger.' The tar stuck on the rabbit's hand and the more he tried to shake it loose, the more he was stuck. So the wolf came up to him and said, 'Well Brer Rabbit, I got you now!'

"Brer Rabbit looked up at him and said, 'Brer Wolf, you can boil me and hot water and skin me alive, but whatever you do, please don't throw me in that briar patch.'

"'Briar patch?' said the wolf.

"'That's right. You can chop my feet off and hang me by the neck until I'm dead, but whatever you do, please don't throw me in that briar patch.'

"The wolf said, 'Don't throw you in the briar patch eh, well one for the money, two for the show, three to get ready, and four to go,'" Ernie motioned as if he was throwing a football to illustrate this action, and after he made a throwing gesture, Ernie looked up in the air and made a whistling sound to symbolize the rabbit flying through the air and made a thumping sound in his mouth to illustrate the rabbit landing in the briar patch before he continued with the tale.

"The rabbit looked up and said, 'Hey Mr. Wolf, you forgetting something.'

"What's that?"

"The rabbit said, 'You forget that I was born and raised in this briar patch and number two, I is a free man now!'

"The wolf smacked himself on his head and carried himself on home. When he got there, his wife said, 'Well, where is it?' The wolf said, 'Honey, we ain't having no rabbit stew tonight.'"[34]

THE WOLF, THE HOUSE AND THE WELL

The Wolf's wife went to Br'er Rabbit and told him that the wolf was dead and he must come and see if he couldn't do some good for him (that was the plan they made to catch the rabbit). Br'er Rabbit went there and stood up in the door and told the wolf's wife that the only good he could do for Br'er Wolf was that Br'er Wolf must get up and walk around the house three times and fall down, then he could tell him whether he could help him for sure or not.

So the wolf got up out of his bed and walked around the house three times, and fell on the ground. At that, Br'er Rabbit jump out of the house and asked the wolf's wife, "How could a dead man walk around the house three times?"

So after the wolf found he couldn't catch him that way, he sent word to Br'er Rabbit's wife to tell her she must send Br'er Rabbit around to help him dig a well, and he wouldn't bother him again. But Br'er Rabbit sent his answer, "No, he don't want not well. He can drink out of a cow's track."

So Br'er Wolf went and dug a well by himself, but the next day when he went there, he saw that the well was almost dry. And he saw some tracks where somebody been to the well and carried all the water. The tracks belonged to Br'er Rabbit.[35]

THE WOLF, THE HOG AND THE LION

The wolf wanted to eat the hog, and didn't know how to get him.

Well the lion had a sick child. He went out hunting for a doctor for the child, and then he meet up with the wolf and the hog, and inquired of them what was good for the sick child.

Then the wolf said to the hog, "Oh Br'er Hog, the lion come to you to ask of you know what's good for the child, because he knows you're a doctor, learned in all the doings of doctors; and instead of you telling him what's good for his child, you take it for a joke to laugh at." And as he said that, the lion got in a passion and was ready to tear up the hog.

So the hog fell down on the ground and told him, "No Br'er Lion, I didn't laugh; it's my teeth that set out of my mouth so. But I can tell you what's good for your sick child." So the hog said to the lion, "You go on home, Br'er Lion, and get a piece of wolf's liver and roast it until it's half done, and if that doesn't cure your child when you're done giving it to him, I'll pay you a hundred dollars."

So the lion said, "Well Br'er Wolf, since you're a wolf, I can go no further to seek for a wolf's liver. I must have a piece of yours."

So the lion fell on the wolf and tore him in pieces, and took the liver home and roast it like the hog told him, fed it to the child, and sure enough, the fever left the child.

Now you see he wanted to take the hog's life, now the hog went and took the wolf's life.

And so you see, the hog's teeth stand out to this day just like he's laughing.[36]

GOD ABOVE

One night the rabbit was in jail and sentenced to hang for stealing food from other people's gardens, so his friend the crane came to visit him. The crane felt sorry for the rabbit, so the rabbit hatched a plan.

The next day, everybody came to the gallows to watch them hang the rabbit. They were about to put the rope around the rabbit's neck when he looked up and said, "Lord, tell these people I ain't guilty." All of a sudden, a voice came from the clouds and said, "That rabbit ain't done nothing! Turn him loose!"

The crowd got scared and ran away from the gallows. Right after that, the crane flew down from behind the clouds, untied the rabbit, and the rabbit said, "Good job, Brother Crane!"

—Maria Middleton[37]

IN THE WELL

Once upon a time a fox was in the well, and a goat came along.

The fox said to the goat, "This water is so nice and cool down here, come down and take a drink!"

So the goat jumped into the well with the fox to get some of the cool water. The fox said to the goat, "Come close up side the well, and let me get on your back and jump out! Then I will help you out." The goat came close up side the well, and the fox jumped out, but he didn't look to see whether the goat could get out or not.[38]

WAIT UPON THE LORD

One day the buzzard sat up on the stake. Br'er Hawk came along and said, "Good morning Br'er Buzzard! What you waiting here for?" The buzzard replied, "Waiting for something to eat." The buzzard asked, "Are you hungry?" "Yes, I'm hungry," replied the hawk. Br'er Buzzard said, "See that sparrow over yonder sitting up there on a sharp stick? Go ahead and catch him and get something to eat." Br'er Hawk darted at the sparrow, who flew away while the hawk was fastened onto the stick. Br'er Buzzard got ready to eat the hawk and said, "It's a good thing to wait on the Lord!"

—Henry Middleton[39]

Brother Rabbit and Brother Wolf decided to plant together one year. So now Brother Rabbit say, "Let us plant potatoes!"

After they through planting, and time to harvest, he said, "Now, Brother Wolf, you take the tops, and give me the bottom." And Brother Wolf agree with this. And the next year they plant peas.

So Brother Rabbit say, "Now, Brother Wolf, last year we plant potato, and I take the bottom and give you the top; so now we plant peas, you must take the bottom now, and give me the tops, and we will be even." "All right!" exclaim old Wolf.

And the next year they plant peanuts; and Brother Rabbit said, "Let me have the bottom, and you take the tops." The next time they plant corn; and the old schemy rabbit then said, "Let me have the tops now, and you take the bottom, and we will be even."

So, after all, the rabbit get all the foods, an' the wolf get the stalks

—Justine Brow[40]

Once upon a time Brer Rabbit and Brer Buzzard sign a degree not to eat for two weeks. You know that Brer Rabbit he is very tricky. He shut the buzzard up, and went home and eat his supper. And come back and say, "I am starving, starving, all the day long." So Brer Buzzard say, "I am starving, starving, the whole day." Brer Rabbit went back, and come the next day and say, "I am starving the whole day long." Buzzard was starved to death. So Brer Rabbit said, "He will not eat me."

That was the end.

—Laura A. Younge[41]

THE FOX AND THE GOOSE

This tale, collected in 1913, may be viewed as an allegory about how the segregation laws that were passed at the time violated the Constitutional rights of Black South Carolinians.

One day a fox was going down the road and saw a goose. "Good morning, Goose," he said; and the goose flew up on a limb and said, "Good morning, Fox."

Then the fox said, "You ain't afraid of me, are you?" Haven't you heard of the meeting up at the other night?"

"No Fox, what was that?"

"They passed a law that no animal must hurt no other animal. Come down and let me tell you about it. The hawk mustn't catch the chicken and the dog mustn't chase the rabbit and the lion mustn't hurt the lamb."

"Is that so?"

"Yes, all live friendly together. Come down and don't be afraid."

As the goose was about to fly down, way off in the woods they heard a "Woo woo! Woo woo!" and the fox looked around.

"Come down, Goose," he said.

And the dog got closer, "Woo woo!"

Then the fox started to sneak off. And the goose said, "Fox, you ain't scared of the dog, are you? Didn't all the animal pass a law at the meeting not to bother each other no more?"

"Yes," replied the fox, "But some of the animals around here don't got no respect for the law."[42]

THE FOX AND THE CAT

The fox said that he had many tricks to help himself in times of trouble. The cat said he had only one trick. Shortly after they discussed the matter, they saw the dog coming. The cat ran up the tree and the dog barked and barked at her, but he couldn't catch her.

The fox tried all ten of his tricks, but after all, the dog caught the fox. So the cat said, "One good trick is better than ten ones that ain't so good."[43]

BR'ER RABBIT EATS BR'ER WOLF

Once upon a time, Br'er Rabbit and Br'er Wolf went fishing. Br'er Wolf got wet up and Br'er Rabbit said, "Br'er Wolf let me dry first." So Br'er Rabbit went in the oven and he dried. When he dried, he came out and said, "Br'er Wolf, you go in now and dry, and when you done dried, you knock."

Br'er Wolf dried off and he knocked the door. Br'er Rabbit said, "You ain't dry yet!" Br'er Wolf knocked again. Br'er Rabbit said, "Oh man, you ain't dry yet!"

Br'er Rabbit opened the door and Br'er Wolf was dead, so Br'er Rabbit and his children had Br'er Wolf for supper.[44]

MAN IN LIQUOR

Once upon a time, there was a cat and a rat. There was a barrel of whiskey. And the rat fell head over heels into the barrel of whiskey. So the rat say, "O Lord! I wish somebody would come by to help me get out my trouble!" And during the time the cat happen to pass by. So the rat say to the cat, "O Br'er Cat! Look yere a minute!"

He say, "Br'er Cat, old feller, if you help me out this barrel of whiskey, you can put me on the grass and let me dry. And after I dry, you can eat me."

And the cat say, "All right." The cat took the rat out, and lay by while he was drying. During the time the rat was drying in the sun, the cat dropped asleep. While the cat was sleeping, the rat slipped in his hole.

Then the cat say, "Ah, Br'er Rat! That ain't the bargain."

So the rat say, "Br'er Cat, old feller, you know when a man in liquor, he say any old thing!"

—Henrietta Johnson[45]

5

Anecdotes of Black Orators

The Black leaders in South Carolina skillfully used the art of storytelling to enhance their oratory. During the Reconstruction era, they often told stories to plead for the rights they were often denied.

Bishop Richard Harvey Cain, best known as the founding pastor of Charleston's Mother Emanuel AME Church, argued for the passage of a South Carolina Constitution that would allow equal rights for all in this speech from February 17, 1868.

> The clock had struck two, and I had dashed down my pen when the thought struck me it might be misunderstood. I retraced my steps and so shaped the petition as simply to state the poor of any class. I bore in mind the poor whites of the upper districts. I saw, not long ago, a poor white woman walk eighteen miles barefooted to receive a bag of corn and four pounds of meat, resting all night on the roadside, eating one-half and then go away, living on roots afterwards and half starved. I desire that class of people to have homes as well as the black man. I have lost long since that hateful idea that the complexion of a man makes any difference as far as rights are concerned. The true principle of progress and civilization is to recognize the great brotherhood of man, and a man's wants, whatever he may be, or whatever clime he comes from, are as sacred to me as any other class of men. I believe this measure will advance the interests of all classes.[46]

Bishop Cain used similar anecdotal skills on January 10, 1874, to argue for a civil rights bill before Congress.

> Sir, the gentleman states that in the State of North Carolina the colored people enjoy all their rights as far as the highways are concerned; that in the hotels, and in the railroad cars, and in the various public places of resort, they have all the rights and all the immunities accorded to any other class of citizens of the United States. Now, it may not have come under his observation, but it has under mine, that such really is not the case; and the reason why I know and feel it more than he does is because my face is painted black and his is painted white. We who have the color—I may say the objectionable color—know and feel all this. A few days ago, in passing from South Carolina to this city, I entered a place of public resort where hungry men are fed, but I did not dare—I could not without trouble—sit down to the table. I could not sit down at Wilmington or at Weldon without entering into a contest, which I did not desire to do. My colleague [Mr. Elliott], the gentleman who so eloquently spoke on this subject the other day, a few months ago entered a restaurant at Wilmington and sat down to be served, and while there a gentleman stepped up to him and said, "You cannot eat here." All the other gentlemen upon the railroad as passengers were eating there; he had only twenty minutes, and was compelled to leave the restaurant or have a fight for it. He showed fight, however, and got his dinner; but he has never been back there since. Coming here last week I felt we did not desire to draw revolvers and present the bold front of warriors, and therefore we ordered our dinners to be brought into the cars, but even there we found the existence of this feeling; for, although we had paid a dollar a piece for our meals, to be brought by the servants into the cars, still there was objection on the part of the railroad people to our eating our meals in the cars, because they said we were putting on airs. They refused us in the restaurant, and then did not desire that we should eat our meals in the cars, although we paid for them. Yet this was in the noble State of North Carolina.
>
> Mr. Speaker, the colored men of the south do not want the adoption of any force measure. No; they do not want anything by force. All they ask is that you will give them, by statutory enactment

under the fundamental law, the right to enjoy precisely the same privileges accorded to every other class of citizens.[47]

Joseph H. Rainey of Georgetown, South Carolina, added his voice to support this bill on February 3, 1875.

It may be true that in Virginia they have some regard for the colored people, but I can mention a circumstance from my personal observation which does not show regard for the dead and little for the living. When in Richmond some two or three years ago I was taken to the outskirts of the city where there was a burial ground in which the slaves had formerly been buried. To my astonishment I found that graveyard cut through for the purpose of opening a street, and the city carts hauling away the dust of those poor dead slaves and strewing the same about the streets to fill up the low places and mud-holes. I saw this with my own eyes, and therefore can testify before God and man as to the fact. Does not this statement show that with some people there is no regard for the poor Negro, living or dead? Think of it! The sacred dust of the dead in a civilized community used to fill up mud-holes and low places!

Yet you talk about humanity; your kindly feeling for the colored race. Gracious Heaven! If you have no feelings for the ashes of the dead; if you have no regard for the dust of the dead slave who served you all the days of his life faithfully, honestly, well, we may have apprehensions as to the manner in which we will be treated, now that we are free and struggling for equal rights, unless we are protected by the strong arm of the law.

We do not intend to be driven to the frontier as you have driven the Indian. Our purpose is to remain in your midst an integral part of the body-politic. We are training our children to take our places when we are gone.

We desire this bill that we nay train them intelligently and respectably, that they may thus be qualified to be useful citizens in their day and time. We ask you, then, to give us every facility, that we may educate our sons and our daughters as they should be. Deprive us of no rights belonging to us as citizens; give us an equal opportunity in life, then if we fail we will be content if driven to the wall.[48]

Robert Browne Elliot of Charleston used this biblical story in support of the same bill.

> The results of the war, as seen in Reconstruction, have settled forever the political status of my race. The passage of this bill will determine the civil status, not only of the negro, but of any other class of citizens who may feel themselves discriminated against. It will form the capstone of that temple of liberty, begun on this continent under discouraging circumstances, carried on in spite of the sneers of monarchists and the cavils of pretended friends of freedom, until at last it stands in all its beautiful symmetry and proportions, a building the grandest which the world has ever seen, realizing the most sanguine expectations and the highest hopes of those who, in the name of equal, impartial, and universal liberty, laid the foundation stones.

> The Holy Scriptures tell us of an humble handmaiden who long, faithfully, and patiently gleaned in the rich fields of her wealthy kinsman; and we are told further that at last, in spite of her humble antecedents, she found complete favor in his sight. For over two centuries our race had "reaped down your fields." The cries and woes which we have uttered have "entered into the ears of the Lord of Sabaoth," and we are at last politically free. The last vesture only is needed—civil rights. Having gained this, we may, with hearts overflowing with gratitude, and thankful that our prayer has been granted, repeat the prayer of Ruth: "Entreat me not to leave thee, or to return from following after thee; for whither thou goest, I will go; and where thou lodgest, I will lodge; thy people shall be my people, and thy God my God; where thou diest, will I die, and there will I be buried; the Lord do so to me, and more also, if aught but death part thee and me."[49]

On February 22, 1948, a Spartanburg minister named Reverend Joel L. King spoke to his congregation at Mt. Moriah Baptist Church about President Harry S. Truman's civil rights proposals and the refusal of southern governors to comply. He used the following anecdote in a fashion similar to that of his more famous nephew, Martin Luther King Jr., several years later.

Here in South Carolina, Negroes are excluded from the polls. We don't want to be a part of the white man's social life, but we do want to vote and have equal educational rights. This bill by President Truman would cure the ills of the South for both whites and Negroes. As is said in Isaiah 28:20, "The bed is too short and the covering narrower than a man can wrap himself up in it." And concluded, the blanket is too small, for South Carolina and the Negroes are left conspicuously from its covering.[50]

6
Profiles and Narratives

Many of these accounts are from the unpublished South Carolina Negro Writers' Project, which was intended to provide a panoramic view of Black life in that state. These were deposited at the University of South Carolina and are now in the public domain, but they have rarely been seen in print. The last two accounts were written by this author.

THE CHARLESTON INSURRECTION: CONTROVERSIES OF ORIGIN AND RESULT

The only insurrection that amounted to anything occurred in 1919, just after the World War. Although it lasted no more than four hours, the city was in the greatest turmoil that words can describe. Men and women of both races who were not in the battle ran here and there for protection. Even the officers of the law got out of the way where the odds were against them.

It started in a restaurant on the corner of Market and Charles Streets about seven o'clock in the afternoon. The restaurant was operated by a Greek man named Police that was intended for Negro patronage.

The trouble began when a sailor gave a Negro boy a twenty dollar bill to get him a pint of moonshine. The boy took the money and gave it to his father and did not return. After he did not return, the sailor got angry and told some of the others what happened. They went back to the restaurant and began to beat the Negroes in there who were unaware of the plot and the cause of the action. Everything breakable that was in sight was hurled from right to left by both Negroes and sailors. When the news went out in the Negro community what was happening, armed men came running through the streets with knives, hammers, hatchets, guns, razors, and sticks and joined whole heartedly into the fight. Young Negroes and white boys who were eager for excitement entered and fought until they had been beaten enough or had been exhausted.

Men were like savages; they screamed to the top of their voices in the middle of the streets. Frantic men and women who did not know what to do or where to go seeked protection in other areas of the city. Every front door was locked, every gate bolted and shutters closed. The mad throng which included some Negro women threw bricks at everything that looked like glass—smashing doors and windows as if a tornado had been passing that way. Feet of men were like the feet of horses on a battlefield, dashing amid shot and shell.

When I heard the screaming and shouts of the men, I went on top of our shed in the back of the yard and heard the crashing of glass as they were coming out of Charles Street and into Beaufain. After they entered Beaufain, I bolted our door and went into the yard to put the bolt on the gate, but before doing that I peeped in the street and on doing so, on the opposite side of the street was an officer hiding in a shack in an open lot. When he saw me, out of the shack he came running toward our gate and yelling at the same time, "Let me in for God's sake. I can't leave my beat but I can't stay in the street!" I did not admit him, but before closing in his face, I said: "You are the one to protect me, not I you." With that, he trotted back to his hiding place, and I bolted the gate from the outside world.

A plainclothes man was given orders from headquarters to stop every car that Negroes occupied and search for guns. This he did, then the acting Chief came and asked if he were not told to stop and search every Negro car for weapons. He replied, "Yes, sir, but every car I stopped were filled with revolvers and guns that were pointed directly at me!"

—James Holloway[51]

EX-CONGRESSMAN THOMAS EZEKIEL MILLER

The Honorable T.E. Miller, 78 Radcliffe Street, Charleston, South Carolina, has served as representative of South Carolina during the period of Reconstruction, He was born in Ferrebeeville, Beaufort County, South Carolina, June 17, 1849. He attended the Charleston public school for free Negroes, and public school in Hudson, New York, and was graduated from Lincoln University in Chester County, Pennsylvania, in 1872. He studied law at the South Carolina College, and was graduated in the last class before Negroes were barred. After graduation he was admitted to the South Carolina bar in 1875, and practiced law in Beaufort, South Carolina.

In 1872, he was appointed school commissioner of Beaufort County, South Carolina, and a member of the state house of representatives from 1872 to 1878, then became a member of the State Executive Committee in 1878, and remained until 1880, after which he served in the state senate. He successfully contested as a Republican the election of William Elliot to the Fifty-First Congress, and served from September 24, 1890, to March 3, 1891, but was an unsuccessful candidate for the Fifty-Second Congress in 1890, and again a member of the state house of representatives in 1894. In 1895, he became a member of the state constitutional convention.

His mother died when he was nine years of age, and at ten had to work for a living. There has been no encouragement by relatives that he was ambitious to continue his schooling, but by friends. The friends who encouraged his going to school were Mr. Giibert Pittsbury, first Republican mayor in Charleston, and Major C.S. Gadsden, vice-president of the Atlantic Coast-Line system. He got a job under Mr. Hart, editor of the *Charleston Mercury*, at the age of ten as distributing salesman of the *Mercury* to the hotels in the city. The hotels were: The Planters, Charleston, Pavillion, Mills House, and St. George. The following year, he was placed in charge of delivering the paper to all stations between Charleston and Savannah, Georgia, on the Savannah Railroad, and remained in service until 1864, when he was made assistant conductor of the railroad. He wore the Confederate uniform, for all public works were owned and operated by the federal government. In the early part of 1865, the train was captured by the Yankees to the south of Harleyville, and he was placed into prison in the stockade river swamp, at Savannah, Georgia, and remained there for two weeks. The few persons survived were moved to the Savannah Hospital, where he also went. When he was released from the hospital, he went to Hilton Head, en route to Harts Island, New York, with the New

York Twenty-Fourth Negro Regiment, and from there to Hudson, New York, and returned to Charleston in 1866.

Dr. Miller's parents were very religious and strict in their protestant doctrines. It was from his mother's teachings and early encouragements that he strived so hard to accomplish some of her dreams. The only chances that came into his life was foresight, and the determination to grasp every opportunity that came within his reach.

After leaving college to practice law in Beaufort, South Carolina, his first client was D.H. Wall, a young merchant in Beaufort County, and remained on his payroll for fifty years as his attorney. Mr. Wall died in 1935, and in his last will and testament, requested of his relatives to keep him as the estate attorney. He is and has been the only to settle any matters concerning the estate, which is worth $200,000. The record is in the Jasper Courthouse, Jasper County.

One of his first political fights in Charleston was to put Negro teachers in the city public schools there, of which he was successful. The committee that he headed was composed of the following persons: Dr. J.A. McFall; Dr. J.M. Thompson; Reverend N.B. Sterrett; I. Edwards, contractor; Mrs. Susan Dart Butler; and Edwin A. Harleston.

In 1876 two parties arose in the legislature; the Mackey and Wallace Houses. Mackey, the Republican, was elected as the head of that party to keep the Democrats from entering the state house. When the Democrats sought entrance into the house and were denied unless they had a certificate from the secretary of state, they then organized themselves and elected Wallace as speaker at the Carolina Hall. At this time it was known as the dual government [legislature]. Miller was a member of the Mackey House and floor manager of the same.

When the members of the Wallace House gained entrance, Wallace demanded that Mackey leave the rostrum, and if it were not for the guards, there would have been bloodshed.

It was Benjamin Tillman who compromised with him to leave national politics. After his retirement, The State A and M College for Negroes at Orangeburg, South Carolina, was founded, and he was made president and remained there fifteen years. The charter for the college was issued by Tillman and friends from the state the latter part of 1894 and first part of 1895.

He has written and ready for the press a true history of Congressional Reconstruction and the part Negroes played in it in South Carolina; also a volume proving that the seed of Tillmanite Revolution was planted in South Carolina by members of the Church of England ten years after which the organization was formed. The volume tells about the rich heritage of Tillman's family. He has short stories ready for publication.

Many difficulties arose in his life, over which he rose. By his unselfish attitude has made many friends, and enemies as well. One of the main things he had to be aware of was the "common elements" in the party of which he was allied. There have been two political investigations and in each case, nothing was found to block his successes as a politician.

His people on his white father's side were and are very wealthy. During the Civil War, he owned millions. His mother is said to be the daughter of Judge Thomas Heyward, one of the signers of the Declaration of Independence.

In settling his Crimball home, he has divided it into three parts, namely: Old House, Preference and Good Hope. The Old House, he has dedicated to the Heyward family as a cemetery, in Beaufort, South Carolina. Congress has appropriated a monument to the family, which was erected there.

Through the course of his life, was never selfish but self-reliant. "Any man or woman," he said, "who is unselfish, self-reliant, industrious, and faithul to every trust, will succeed in life."

He has never chewed tobacco or smoked, but used alcoholic drinks in a moderate manner.

He is a member of Zion Presbyterian Church, Charleston, South Carolina, of which his mother was a member.

On account of blindness, the honorable gentleman has retired to private life, and spends his time with one of his daughters, writing about his experiences through life, and the things that made his living a success.[52]

MARY WRIGHT, SLAVE-BORN EDUCATOR, SPARTANBURG, SOUTH CAROLINA

For fifty-eight years, Mary Wright has lived a life of service, having taught in the Spartanburg County Negro Schools. She began teaching in a brush arbor near Inman, South Carolina, and now is accredited with being the founder of the city's Leading Negro School, the Carrier Street School, and is a leader in religious and charity work among Negroes.

Mary Wright never stopped looking for ways to serve. A few years ago, she became interested in playground work, and since then has made it a hobby that undoubtedly has done great work for Negro children. She believed in being prepared. When she decided to engage in playground leadership, she went to Washington, attended the District of Columbia school for playground supervisors, and observed the work of the playgrounds of the city.

Mary Wright was born a slave just before the close of the Civil War. Her parents belonged to the Wilson family on South Church Street. Her father was not educated, but he had great respect for education. When an opportunity presented itself to send his little girl to school, he did it, and later managed to send her for a year to Claflin College at Orangeburg, South Carolina.

Mary Wright's first schooling was received in a house converted into a school on the site of the Spartanburg Herald Journal Building. It was conducted by a Mr. and Mrs. Pool (White) who came down from the North right after the war with a zeal to educate the Negroes. "They were Yankees, but they were not carpetbaggers," Mary Wright said. "Their aim was to give the South something and not take it away." She so admired the learning of Mr. and Mrs. Pool and their desire to divide it, she was imbued with the [drive] to serve right off and began at the age of nine, teaching a Sunday school class in the Methodist church.

The year after she attended Claflin College in 1878, she was engaged to teach in the brush arbor near Inman. A short time later, a log schoolhouse was erected for her. Later, she taught in the town of Inman.

While she only attended college one year, Mary Wright has been a student all her life. She has kept up with the trends in teaching by home study, and was awarded a first class life certificate in 1921.

Mary Wright began teaching in Spartanburg in a residence known as the old Chaplin home. A few years later, she founded the Carrier Street School, "a monument of joy," as she expressed it.

Her work has not been confined to the schoolroom. She has been chairman of the Negro division of the County Red Cross Chapter since the [First] World War. She founded a home on Cudd Street for aged Negro women, which is also used for a day nursery and Bible school. She is chairman of the Christmas tree committee for needy children and has been on the county fair committee since 1931.

Mary Wright hasn't been content with educating thousands of other people's children but has educated her own. She sent four daughters and three sons through the public schools of Spartanburg and some of them to college. All of her daughters became teachers, one son is an undertaker in Boston, Massachusetts. Another a shoemaker in Washington, and a third was a bicycle mechanic for fifteen years, prior to his death in Washington where he engaged in the same work.

With the Carrier Street School as a "monument to her joy," Mary Wright's reward for being a good and faithful public servant and doing things well includes the willing respect of thousands of Spartanburg citizens. "I seldom whip a child, though I do have a switch," she stated. "Sometimes I shame a child into behaving."

—Interview by Hattie Mobley of the
South Carolina Negro Writers' Project

Mary H. Wright died in 1946. In a 1944 article in the Spartanburg Herald Journal, *Mrs. Wright was quoted as saying that she would stop teaching "when I'm dead child—I reckon when I'm dead." She also said, "The fellow who has a good education and no manners is half crazy and the fellow with no education, but good manners is intelligent." In 2020, the City of Spartanburg celebrated Mrs. Wright's birthday. Hazel Jackson, who was one hundred years old at the time, told Chris Lavender of the* Spartanburg Herald Journal, *on August 12, 2020, of her recollections of Mrs. Wright. "We learned a lot and studied the word of God and got a good education. We prayed every morning. The Lord's Prayer was taught every morning. It was a great thing because we got to pray and love each other." James Talley, who was the first Black mayor of Spartanburg in the 1990s, referred to Mrs. Wright as "the mother of education for the Black community."*[53]

JOHN WESLEY SEXTON

Let it be said to begin that John Wesley Sexton, MD, of Spartanburg is a remarkable man. Struggling up from a place of obscurity to a position of prominence and success, he has pointed the way by which others may succeed. He is not afraid of the truth about himself or his race. He believes in seeking the truth about a situation and then facing it fearlessly. If there are difficulties, let them be overcome by courage and energy. These are the qualities that have made Dr. Sexton a leader in almost every department of life among his people.

Here is a mere narrative of his life. He was born at Honea Path, January 4, 1876. His parents were Wesley T. Sexton, a licensed preacher and farmer, and Martha (Mattison) Sexton. His grandfathers were Ben Sexton and George Hamp. He first attended public school at Honea Path and later the graded high school at the same place. He graduated from the Agricultural College in 1899 and took his medical course at Leonard College, Shaw University, winning his MD in 1906. On June 9 of the same year, he was married to Lula Bell Crout, daughter of Oscar and Julia Crout, of Laurens. She bore him three children: John Wesley Jr., Lula Bell and Helen May. He began practice at Conway, Arkansas, but later located at Spartanburg, where he has built up a good general practice and established a prosperous drug business under the style of Piedmont Drug Store.

Dr. Sexton remembers with gratitude the constant efforts of his father to direct his feet in the proper paths of industry and economy. His father helped him through public school, but after that he had to work his way. After school was out, he would return to the farm and work at seven dollars per month to repay what his father had lent him. He was enterprising and learned the barber's trade and made this help him also. Later when he entered the State College and learned to be a bricklayer and plasterer, his earning capacity was further enhanced. So when he went to Leonard, he was able to support himself by the addition of what he learned at his trade during vacation.

Dr. Sexton has not done things by halves. He has attended Sunday school all his life. He joined the church when he was ten years old and made clerk. He has been an active member since and has been superintendent of the Sunday school and deacon of the Mt. Moriah Baptist Church.

He has entered into politics in the same whole-hearted way. He was chairman of the Spartanburg county committee, and in 1914, when the party wanted to put forward a man to voice its sentiments to the Fourth South Carolina District, he accepted the nomination for Congress and issued an address which is a strong political document.

In business it is the same. He not only conducts a successful business of his own, but is local president of the Negro Business League and seeks in every legitimate way to teach his people cooperation.

In all matters pertaining to race conditions, he takes an advanced, intelligent position. He keeps in close and sympathetic touch with race conditions through the papers and believes in setting forth conditions as they are and contending earnestly for every right of citizenship. Summed up in a word, he asks for simple justice and a square deal, and what he asks for himself and his race, he stands ready to grant to every other man and every other race. He believes in intelligent religious leadership whose message shall be related to the problems and plans of this life, as well as the life to come.

Among the secret orders he belongs to are the Masons, The Pythians, Odd Fellows, and Working Benevolents, in all of which he is prominent.

He tells a characteristic story about himself. When he was eighteen, he had about decided to buy a mule and buggy and settle down on the farm. Once, when visiting his best girl, who was a student at Spelman Seminary and who had another suitor, a student from Atlanta Baptist College, Dr. Sexton was embarrassed and angered when they laughed at his ungrammatical language. As a result, he abandoned the idea of the mule and buggy and decided to complete his education. With what success that was done the foregoing sketch will show.[54]

CELIA DIAL SAXON

For fifty-five years, Celia Dial Saxon, the most beloved and outstanding woman in all South Carolina, labored earnestly in the fields of education and social improvement in Columbia and the entire state. Her sudden death on January 29, 1935, cast its shadow all over South Carolina. Thousands of people knew her intimately; many had passed directly under her influence in the classroom; others worked with her in community uplift. Both races realized her worth and loved and respected her for her fine spirit of cooperation.

Born a slave seventy-eight years ago, Celia Saxon spent her entire life in Columbia, giving generously of herself and her talents. She was reared by her grandmother Jane Ballard, who made the way brighter for her childhood by tireless effort and constant encouragement. Even as a small child, she was intensely interested in school. On every occasion, she took advantage of educational opportunities offered Negroes. She attended small private schools conducted in the city, the old Howard School, then in charge of white teachers from the North, and Benedict College.

At that time, Negro students were admitted to the South Carolina College. Celia Saxon, with her burning desire for an education yet unquenched, enrolled and in 1877 was graduated from the Normal School of the South Carolina College, now the University of South Carolina. During her student days at this institution, she came under the influence of Mr. William Warren of Connecticut, then a teacher at the college. It was his fine teaching and exemplary character, which caused her to enter the teaching profession. Mr. Warren's maxims she carried always in her classroom and daily life.

Almost all of her teaching experience was in Columbia. Her first work was at the old Howard School under the superintendency of the late Dr. D.B. Johnson, whom afterwards became president at Winthrop College. In her fifty-five years in the classroom, she worked hand in hand with superintendents and principals. In this long period of service, she was absent only three times and never tardy.

With all her students, Celia Saxon struggled hard, encouraging bright students, making the way easier for slower boys and girls, and begging with tears in her eyes the irresponsible to change their ways. She felt peculiarly near to many children because she had taught their parents before them.

As marks of esteem, the Columbia School Board awarded her a gold medal for not being absent or tardy for twenty-five years and, in 1930, named the Saxon School on Blossom Street in her honor. The State Agricultural and Mechanical College at Orangeburg, realizing her splendid contribution to society, awarded her an honorary master of arts degree in 1926.

Celia Saxon was also interested in the organization for self-improvement and took active part in professional organizations, city, state and national. For thirty years, she served as treasurer of the Palmetto State Teachers Association and upon several occasions represented that body at the national meetings.

Besides her untiring efforts in the classroom, Mrs. Saxon was extremely interested in community welfare. She was deeply concerned over the welfare of women and girls and gave her time freely to their problems. She was active first in the development of a working girls' home. Seeing the desirability of turning this effort to national account, she with other club women affiliated and formed the Phyllis Wheatley branch here. The building at Park and Hampton Streets, purchased largely through her efforts, stands as a permanent memorial. For many years, she served as president of this body and, at her death, was serving as a trustee. Other clubs in Columbia of which she was the organizer were the Culture Club, the Lend a Hand Club, and The Women's Christian Temperance Union branch. She was one of the pillars of the State Federation for Colored Women's Clubs, serving as treasurer for many years. Continuing her interest in girls and women, she was one of the founders of the Fairwold Home for Orphans at Cayce, South Carolina. When the City of Columbia and the legislature of South Carolina failed to provide funds for the continuance of the work at the Fairwold

Home, Mrs. Saxon and the other clubwomen of the federation were not discouraged. Instead, they worked harder and made more substantial contributions to the institution, and induced others who were not members of the body to make donations.

On the day of her funeral, the body lay in state in the auditorium of the Booker Washington High School while thousands of sorrowing students and former students of the school and friends passed the bier.

In half a century, thousands of boys and girls have come under the influence of this great woman. Many of them are now men and women making their contributions to society, their lives richer for having made such a powerful contact. The *Columbia State* in an editorial said that "her services were not confined to the four walls of the classroom as evidenced by her active participation in educational and welfare movements. Her devotion to her work and her loyalty to the high ideals of her profession have merited the emulation not only of the members of her race, but of all who are engaged in the important business of guiding the young."

Her place in the school and the community was filled so well that there is no need for refilling. However, she left a heritage to the students, teachers and community workers the great responsibility of carrying on the tasks she so nobly performed.[55]

J.B. MAXWELL: AN EX-SLAVE'S STORY

Many of the best stories from the slavery era have been forever lost to the graveyards, because too often, many of those who remembered and lived through them were unable to write them. Fortunately, there were some who listened. Some were willing to preserve them to inspire future generations. This is one such story.

As I grew up, my mother, Pearl Maxwell Fordham, who died in 2014 at the age of ninety-one, and other elders would occasionally tell stories about being raised by her legendary grandfather James Buchanan "J.B." Maxwell. Born in slavery in Flat Rock, North Carolina, to Jackson and Selina Maxwell in 1854, he was enslaved by a James Maxwell who also owned a plantation in that area. After emancipation, according to generations of family lore, J.B. and his family literally walked from Flat Rock to the Four Mile section of

Mount Pleasant, South Carolina, to be reunited with family members who had been sold to South Carolina.

Around 1873, J.B. managed to attend and graduate from Charleston's Avery Institute, and he would later use his education to help his community. He married Rebecca Mitchell in 1876 and opened up a general store in the Four Mile community, across from the present location of Olive Branch AME Church on Highway 17. Mrs. Elizabeth Scott Ellis, who is now in her nineties, recalled being in the store when two "hoodlums" (as J.B. would often refer to them) stole some sausages from the store while she was in the rear of the store getting some thread and needle for her mother. "I was so scared that Mr. J.B. think that I did it that I ran out of the store and did not go back for a long time."

My mother often spoke of J.B. voting when few other Black people did so. In 2015, my cousin Sherryl Washington James, a local librarian, located a document that proved this fact. The Congressional Record of November 12, 1879, included a transcript of a trial regarding Black voters in Mount Pleasant allegedly voting while illiterate. A number of Black individuals took the stand, and cross-examiners embarrassed them by proving that they could not read nor understood the basics of voting or government. However, the transcript shows that when Attorney G.R. Walker called J.B. Maxwell to testify, he shocked the lawyer by showing and proving not only that could he read, but he also knew who and what he was voting for.

J.B. was a proud man who supported his family. During the Great Depression of the 1930s, despite hard times, he refused to allow my grandmother and mother to work. My mother would often tell of how in order to make ends meet, my grandmother would sneak off to Boone Hall Plantation with my mother when J.B. was off at the store, and they would pick tomatoes in the fields to secretly earn extra money. At Boone Hall Plantation today, in the building that used to serve as the commissary, there are pictures of Black people working in the tomato fields during that period.

Along with working and managing the store, J.B. served his community with his education.

He insisted on correct English from his children and grandchildren, as well as the children who came to the store, and would help locals read their mail and legal documents. He was also the first Black notary public in the Mount Pleasant area, and the *Charleston News and Courier* of January 2, 1909, noted that he was asked to read President Lincoln's Emancipation Proclamation at an Emancipation Day celebration in Mount Pleasant. Some years ago, local historian Dorothy Fludd presented me with a document that he notarized on August 22, 1931, regarding a widow's pension for Elizabeth Jenkins, whose husband, Edmund, served in the Union army during the Civil War. As part of the document, J.B. included an interesting sentence that sums up the difficulty of preserving local histories of African Americans during this era: "She cannot furnish evidence of her birth from the public record because they were none kept in those days."

Fortunately, my mother was alive when I was given this document. Upon showing it to her, she smiled and said, "Yeah, that's Papa's handwriting."

The *Charleston Evening Post* of October 8, 1940, reported J.B. Maxwell's death and announced that his funeral would be held the next day at Olive Branch AME Church. He was eulogized in the November 2, 1940 edition of the *Columbia Palmetto Leader* in an article titled "A Great Man Has Fallen," which told his story in detail. If this story inspires those who have grown up with the stories of their ancestors to preserve them, it will have served its purpose.[56]

WALTER HENRY SNYPE: PAPPA'S STORY

There are individuals who do not make the history books but who live such interesting lives that their stories are worth saving from a permanent loss to the cemetery.

March 1973.

I was in the second grade, and as was often the case when my parents were not yet home from work, I went to the home of my mother's best friend, Mrs. Louise Francis, whom I called "Mama Lou." Mama Lou was apparently away at the neighborhood corner store that she ran, but her father, Mr. Walter Snype, whom we all called "Pappa" (rhymes with "Kappa"), was home. However, he was in a condition unlike any I had ever seen him in before.

Pappa was seated in a chair in the living room, draped with the kind of covering one wears when getting their hair cut. The ceiling light shone on his brown bald head, but he was not wearing his usual wire-framed glasses. I noticed that two of his granddaughters, both of whom babysat me when I was younger, were feeding him from a jar of Gerber baby food from a spoon.

"Pappa," I asked, "why is a grown man like you eating Gerber baby food?"

One of the granddaughters told me to be quiet and mind my own business.

At this point, Pappa tried to talk, but only gurgling sounds emerged from his throat.

"Why are you talking so funny, Pappa?" I asked.

At this, one of the granddaughters chased me upstairs. I would learn a few hours later that Pappa had suffered a stroke the night before.

My mother woke me up the next night to tell me that Pappa had passed. In those days, it was considered inappropriate for small children to attend funerals, as it was felt that they would be upset with all of the intense emotionalism on display. So that day in the living room was the last time I ever saw Pappa.

Mr. Walter Henry Snype (1896–1973), whom we called Pappa, was the son of James and Phoebe Snype of Mount Pleasant, South Carolina, and both of his parents were born shortly after the end of slavery. He was a hardworking, respected leader in our community and a man of no nonsense.

My mother recalled hearing from one of his sisters that Pappa's father, James Snype Sr., drowned in a boating accident sometime in the early 1900s, so Pappa raised his younger brothers and sisters in such a manner that they believed he was their father instead of their older brother. He completed a basic education at the Laing School for Black Children in Mount Pleasant. Around the time he married Lottie Canty, he became well known as a local storeowner, handyman, property owner and community leader. During the Great Depression, he operated a local soup kitchen and occasionally took the homeless into his own home for shelter. After Ms. Canty's death in 1965, he married the late Ms. Lucille Funny, whom I referred to as "Miss Lucille" as a child.

He was also known for helping a many people in his community. According to his granddaughter Patricia Francis, he was known for taking in people who were in need of a place to stay. Among these people was my mother, Pearl Maxwell Fordham, whom Pappa partially raised after her grandparents died when she was a teenager. My mother and Pappa's daughter Louise Snype Francis considered each other sisters until the latter's death in 2000. The relationship between our families was such that, as a child, I believed that Pappa was actually my grandfather.

He had a tool shed in the rear of his house, where he constantly worked on items for his household as well as for those in need while smoking his beloved Tampa Nugget cigars. Along with the tools, I remember that he had many books in the shed, which he cheerfully allowed me to borrow. Among the many I read was *Children's Guide to Knowledge*, a sort of single-volume encyclopedia with colorful illustrations that captivated my young mind. There was also *Eyewitness: The Negro in American History*, by William Loren Katz, which mesmerized me with the history I was not getting in school and planted the seeds for my interest in it, and a novel called *Toby Tyler*, about an abused boy who ran away with the circus, which I found quite interesting.

Our relationship was equally interesting. He was known to rant and rave when he was agitated. Two cases I recall include one in which I ate some of his graham crackers without his permission and one in which I tipped over the ashtray with his Tampa Nugget cigar. He was a sight on those occasions. He would huff and puff in the middle of his yelling. Yet while he occasionally spanked his own grandchildren, he never laid a hand on me for some reason. Despite his rough manner, it was clear, even then, that this man had a lot of love for me.

Pappa went on to work at the Charleston Naval Shipyard, where, in 1945, he was honored for inventing a ship caulking device for which he received $200, a princely sum at the time. He was among the founders of his neighborhood's Cub and Boy Scout troop, Troop 107, which lasted over a decade after his death, and he ran a shoe repair shop for a side income. He was also a major leader and trustee of Mount Pleasant's Friendship AME Church, often building and designing materials used in the church long after his death, such as the church's chandelier, and his name is on a marker outside the church. He served in this capacity until a stroke took his life on March 5, 1973, at the age of seventy-seven.

Pappa was one of the first people I was close to who passed away, but as one who never knew any of my grandfathers, I can at least say that I knew Pappa.[57]

The author, in 2023, at the baobab tree in Dakar, Senegal, West Africa, which, according to tradition, is where the griots are buried. *Author's collection*.

Above: The author at the griot statue in Banjul, Gambia, West Africa, 2022. *Author's collection*.

Left: The author with Khady Ba. *Author's collection*.

THE FIRST COLORED SENATOR AND REPRESENTATIVES,
In the 41ˢᵗ and 42ⁿᵈ Congress of the United States

Opposite: Elijah Green at the Slave Market in Charleston, 1941. *Library of Congress*.

Above: Black Congressmen during Reconstruction. Joseph Rainey and Robert Brown Elliot are seated on the far right. *Author's collection*.

Left: Richard Harvey Cain. *Library of Congress*.

Above, left: Ann J. Edwards, the daughter of Richard Harvey Cain, 1938. *Library of Congress.*

Above, right: Thomas Miller and his wife, Anna Miller, 1924. *Library of Congress.*

Right: *Brer Rabbit and the Tar Baby*, by A.B. Frost, 1895. *Library of Congress.*

Above: Black students at the University of South Carolina during Reconstruction. Celia Dial Saxon is believed to be the woman second from the left in the front row. *Courtesy of the University of South Carolina's Caroliniana Library.*

Right: J.B. Maxwell. *Author's collection.*

Friday, August 24, 1945   **PRODUCE TO WIN** — Yard Names and Faces Make News

$9,000 A YEAR SAVED! Put down in cash dollars that's approximately how much money Shipwright Walter Snype's Beneficial Suggestion will save each year. He won the top award, $250, at a recent Beneficial Suggestions Award ceremony held in the Joiner Shop. The suggestion was that an air chipping hammer be used to remove putty and pitch from seams or crevices of wood decks and hulls of ships in preparation for caulking. When the new method is applied, one man can accomplish the same results that formerly required the work of four men.

34 New Shop Members Gr
by CNY Electric Workers

By Mildred Vaughn

Here's the latest list of newcomers who are being welcomed by old-timers into the shop: Arthur C. Edwards, Primus Washington, Furman M. Reynolds, Jr., Ralph N. Todd, Thollie L. Blackstock, Ralph Burns, Fred L. Crawford, Joe H. Williams, James L. Green, Eldon E. Woods.

Harvey C. Anderson, Lee P. Ravenel, Charles L. Bernero, George D. Willard, Samuel White, Edfield White, Hayward C. Johnson, Benjamin Prioleau, Robert L. Mayers, John Calhoun, Kelly Washington, Billy W. Cleveland, Rally F. Buchanan, Henry Richardson.

Reubin Bryant, Anderson H. Smith, John C. Simmons, Richard B. Lawrence, Fred Long, Ray Q. Simmons, Charles P. Motte, James Pinckney, Jr., Maxwell A. Bloe and Adell Carey.

Edward S. Howard has been promoted to leadingman electrician to fill the vacancy created by the retirement of Francis A. King. Mr. King, who at one time acted as yard photographer, had been employed here since 1917.

Members of the Electric Shop were sorry to learn of the death of Lawton W. Smith. A former employee in the shop, he was killed in action overseas. He was in the Army.

Congratulations to Carlos L. Faught and Tarleton S. Moody who have been appointed shop planners. . . . Friends extend get-well wishes to: Wilbert J. Peacock's daughter in Jacksonville; John H. Carter's wife, Wrightville, Ga.; Charlie Lowder's sister, and Lavern C. Moore's wife who are in the hospital here; and to Walter R. Lester's mother and wife.

Reunions with returning servicemen were enjoyed by Keith Kistler and Olin W. Patrick when their brothers returned home from overseas. . . . William Stone also enjoyed a homecoming with his son-in-law who has returned from England. He is in the Army.

Zora T. Jones is spending some time with her parents before enlisting in the SPARs. . . . Word has been received from Argel S. Moon, a former member of the shop. He is now a Petty Officer in a ship repair unit at Bainbridge, Md. Ray England, another former employe in the shop, is also stationed with this group.

Personnel in the Time Office welcome Beatrice Neal. She has been transferred from the Sheetmetal Shop to this office. . . . Marjorie Bonner has returned to work after a vacation with her husband, Darrell, at Fort Sill, Okla.

Co-workers extend their deepest sympathy to Robert L. Gibson in the death of his father-in-law, and to Kelly Washington and Albert Proctor in their recent bereavements.

Personnel
Romance Ru
Two Wed; O

Dan Cupid is b among members of Murray of the Civ was married to Johi ceremony took place The groom is from of Laura Scoggins. Maurice McDaniel a will take place in t town of Olanta, S. signed her position

The engagement lentine to Eugene Mate, third-class, ha

August 14 was a c Marie Leyh. Not . the end of the war her birthday.

Visiting her home Bonnie Drake. . . vacationing in Color ey and Bonnie Stud CNY. Bill will retu Lt. Hugh Ward, Arn Sgt. Julia Kelly, Ma ed the office.

Louise DeLoache join her husband i guerite Sutton will that city with her. iatives there. . . Lou er, James, is a new Yard.

Planning
New System
CNY Job Or

The Job Order Se job orders has ended been established tha section to get out as per day.

This is how it w is alloted a certain a day that must be port is sent to the showing the number typed and left over. jobs exceed a certa pists remain on the out. No job is allov the section over a s time without being duplicated. This re orders moving throu a steady rate of spe

The welcome that Lucia Compton, typi S. C.; Ruth Inabinet Pleasant, S. C.; Gi clerk, Wichita, Kans. stenographer, Charles

Two Army Veterans Begin
Civilian Life in Machine, South

By Laura Munnerlyn

Members of the Machine Shop were especially happy to hang out the welcome sign for two discharged veterans of World War II and welcome them into the trade. They are Robert Larson and Edgar Watson.

Robert, who was in the Army for

Drafting
Drafting Goes Modern
With New Glass Office
By Freddie Puckhaber

There's been quite a bit of moving going on in Drafting in preparation

98

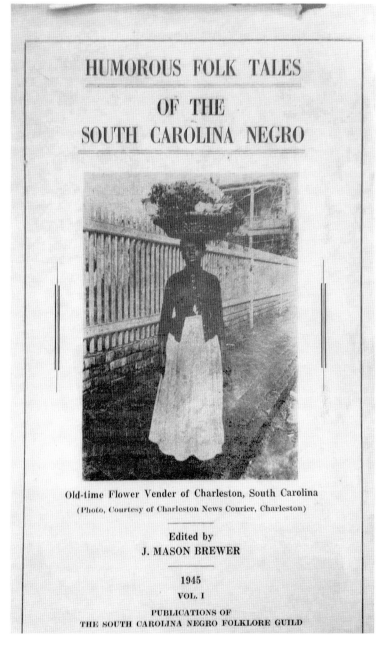

HUMOROUS FOLK TALES

OF THE
SOUTH CAROLINA NEGRO

Old-time Flower Vender of Charleston, South Carolina
(Photo, Courtesy of Charleston News Courier, Charleston)

Edited by
J. MASON BREWER

1945
VOL. I

PUBLICATIONS OF
THE SOUTH CAROLINA NEGRO FOLKLORE GUILD

Humorous Folk Tales of the South Carolina Negro. Courtesy of the Avery Research Center, Charleston, SC.

Top, left: A selection from the journal of Abraham Fordham Jr. *Author's collection.*

Top, right: The autobiography of Abraham Fordham Jr. *Author's collection.*

Bottom, left: Abraham Fordham Jr., 1973. *Author's collection.*

Bottom, right: Pearl Maxwell Fordham, 1975. *Author's collection.*

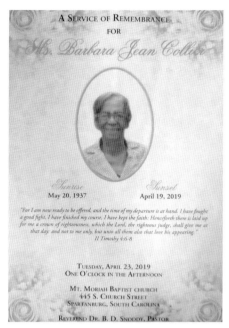

Clockwise from top left: Obituary for Barbara Collier; Obituary for Jesse Montgomery; The author with Joseph Kimpson; The author with Samuel McGowan. *Author's collection.*

The author with children in Senegal, West Africa. *Author's collection.*

7

Forgotten Stories from the Archives

A number of these stories were collected from the South Carolina Negro Writers Project and another project by a Black folklorist named J. Mason Brewer. In 1945, Brewer published a work organized by the South Carolina Negro Folklore Guild titled Humorous Folk Tales of the South Carolina Negro. *Based out of Claflin College in Orangeburg, South Carolina, Brewer's group collected tales from around the state. The fact that most of these stories were told by Black individuals to Black writers adds to the authenticity of the humor. Both works are in the public domain.*

THE SILLY WIFE

Once upon a time, there was a man and wife living in the country. They had a large farm and raised a lot of hogs and cabbages. The man killed half of his hogs and put the meat in a house in the yard. So one day he went to work and told his wife to cook a lot of cabbages and put a lot of meat in it.

The woman didn't quite understand: she went and carried all the meat out of the house to the garden and stuck a piece in each head of cabbage.

In a few minutes, her husband came home hungry. He said, "Give me my dinner." She told him she thought he told her to put the meat in the cabbage in the garden. So the man didn't say nothing.

So the man went back to work next day and told his wife to give the hogs plenty of water. The woman took the hogs one by one and threw them in the well. The man came home again.

So he called the hogs to give them shrill [swill]. No hogs came. So he asked his wife, "Where are the hogs?" She said, "They are in the well. Didn't you tell me to give them water?"

The end.

—Rubertha Polite[58]

GOLD CHEST STORY

A story is told by one as saying that her mother was given the secret of the whereabouts of a chest of gold. When it was time for her to get the chest, two men were hired who carried rods and loadstones to sound the earth for the chest. The instruments have the ability to bring the treasure near to the surface to be heard. This place was in a graveyard. A tombstone was lain flat over the chest with engravings on it as though it were a grave. When the chest was in sight, coming to the surface by the instruments of the treasure gatherers, the women became frightened seeing such a large one, which was said by the spirit to be filled, and said, "Look at the money." The men did not have time to punch a hole in it, for at the utterance of these words, like a flash of lightning it made a sudden jerk—and the velocity of its swiftness seemed to have jarred the whole Earth, and to the very depth of the Earth it went. Fortunately, no harm came to any of them, which was said to be very unusual. From the loss of wealth and remorse of having spoken carried her to an early grave.

—Hagar Campbell[59]

PEEP HELL

A woman once owned a parrot and a canary, which she took great delight in caring for. The canary was a sweet singer and understood her mistress's approvals and disapprovals as though it were an individual. In the early mornings, especially in the spring, it would make the beautiful home more attractive by its melodious notes. The parrot was a great talker. It tried to say anything that was said by its mistress, and her many friends who would always crowd its day stands to hear it rehearse what was said. The parrot was one of the most sensitive of parrots.

One summer's day when the sun poured through with all its might, heat that sent men and beasts wild with madness, the canary and parrot were carried to their respective places on the veranda for the day where they could be free to catch some of the chanced wind that blew and their merriment would be unmolested. This time of the season, men and beasts would resort to the things that would bring relief to their agonized bodies, which have been tormented by the sweltering heat. The family bathroom was on one end of the veranda of which the birds' haven was. The canary sang its beautiful songs and the parrot rehearsed phrases and sentences that were taught and heard directly and indirectly.

At a certain hour each day, the mistress went to the bathroom to make her usual preparation for the day, but had forgotten to close the door on entering, or did not think it mattered. So as she busied herself in the bathroom, the canary continued her music, but the parrot stopped and was looking in the bathroom through the half closed door. On seeing the parrot so still and gazing through the open door the canary began to look, too. After a few moments, the canary in a wee voice said, "Peep peep." The parrot was standing on one foot so long that it changed from one to the other in an unconcerned manner, but eyes still in the room: "Peep—hell, I'm taking a damned good look!"

—Queen Breech[60]

THE LOWCOUNTRY GIRL AND THE LITTLE LAMB

A Lowcountry girl had a little lamb. The girl's name was not Mary; nor did her lamb follow her to school one day, but he was a much loved pet, having been raised on a bottle from birth.

After a time, as the lamb grew it continued to follow its small mistress about. One day, it followed her and her brother to a Negro funeral. The brother became separated from the little girl and the sheep, the open grave being between them. The two children and the sheep stood entranced by the "carryings-on" of the bereft widow, whose husband's body had just been laid into the grave. She screamed and kicked, trying violently to throw herself upon the coffin in the open grave. The strength of three men was required to restrain her from her purpose, and the two children and the sheep enjoyed the scene immensely with three pairs of solemn round eyes.

The small brother, fumbling absently in his pocket during the proceedings came upon a hard round object and drew it forth. It proved to be a raw sweet potato—a delicious delicacy—and he forthwith forgot the widow's grief long enough to take a nibble from the potato. However, there was one to see—the sheep. And a sweet potato also being the sheep's favorite dish, the animal leaped across the open grave in pursuit of the potato and, in doing so, accidentally assisted the Negro woman in accomplishing her ambition to cast herself upon her dead husband's body, for he bumped into her trying to get the potato and knocked her flat upon the coffin.

In a flash, the widow knew that she had got what she didn't want after all, for before anybody could have counted to ten, she was out—and it didn't take even one man to help her get out!

—Victoria Attles[61]

THE MINISTER AND THE BOY

Rowboats were the only means of transportation from one place to another where there were rivers and creeks. Ministers as well as others who had duties to perform in various places located on islands in villages, were transported in the summer. One day, a minister wanted to go from Johns Island to Wadmalaw Island, both in South Carolina, which are not many miles apart, and being the only other passenger in the boat, he ventured into a conversation with a boy.

"Well son," said the minister, "do you go to school?"

"No, sir," said the boy in his rustic manner.

"Have you heard of subjects taught in school such as English, arithmetic, geography, history, French, Latin, sociology, physiology and the many other subjects?"

"Yes," the boy replied, "but I can never go to school; I had to work."

The minister continued his conversation until, when they were gone about midway, a storm came up so suddenly that even the boy who did not know anything of the many subjects the minister asked of but a prize swimmer, was also frightened. The minister became very restless, for he knew he knew his fate if the storm did not subside. But in spite of his voiceless and lamentable prayers, the storm did not. The waves were rolling high, and the boat was getting full by the waves of the turbulent sea. When the minister had gotten too frightened to pray, seeing the boat would go down any minute, the boy said to the minister, "Well Rev., do you know about "swim-ology?" The minister, almost horrified, replied, "No, son, I have never had a lesson in swimming."

"Well," said the boy, "you better get all your 'ologies' together and get on overboard, because I don't know but one 'ology,' and I'm going to use it now." With those words, seeing that the boat was almost full and any moment would be the fatal one, the boy dived into the river and on coming up, looked back at the sinking boat and the minister sitting horrified on his seat. The boy got safely to shore, but the poor minister made his eternal home in the bottom of the sea.

—Mrs. Irene Noisette[62]

THE WHITE MAN AND HIS SERVANT

A gentleman said to his servant, "Jim, go get the buggy and go to Pinckney's and get the mule, and drive down to the store and get the groceries."

The servant replied, "Mister, you tell me to go to three places at the same time. Dog got four legs, but he can just run in one path."[63]

THE DEVIL'S DAUGHTER

Once upon a time, there was a man who had a name, Jack. He had want to marry to the Devil's daughter. He told him the only way he would let him marry to his daughter, if he plant rice an' make it in one day. So the Devil daughter hear them talk about the rice. So the Devil daughter told him how to do it.

So Jack told the rice, "Drop, drop!" So the rice drop. And he told the rice to grow. So the rice grow. And told the rice, "Cut!" So the rice cut. And he told the rice to bunch. And the rice bunch.

And he told the Devil he was through. The Devil give him his daughter, and so Jack got his wife.

—Joseph S. Shanklin[64]

HELL BOUND

The pastor selected for his Sunday night message a very interesting subject, which was "beautiful and rich hell." The ungodly as well as the godly were curious to hear what he had to say on the subject in regard to such a subject as hell. The church was packed that night as it never was, except on special occasions. The pastor painted a vivid picture of hell with Satan as its ruler and the members of his cabinet and their offices. When the picture was completed, he told of the various types of people who have gone there to make their eternal home in the kingdom of the eternal fiend. Continuing his lifelike picture of the place, he said, "There is money in hell; there is liquor in hell; there are pretty women in hell!" Before he could say another word, a man in the audience stood up and interrupted him by asking, "Pastor, did you say money is in hell; liquor is in hell; and pretty women in hell?" The pastor said, "Why yes, those are my exact words." At this time, he had began to push his way out of the seat on which he sat. When he reached the aisle, he said, "Well pastor, you needn't preach any more, I'm hell bound!" And with those words, he disappeared into the darkness of the night.

—Mr. W.S. Noisette[65]

OLD SAYINGS

Young people think old people fool, but old people know young people fool.
Many slip between the cup and the lip.
Don't let the same bee sting you twice.
Never judge a book by the cover.

—Ruby Gomez[66]

It is better to forgive than to revenge.
It is good to begin well, better to end well.
It is more brave to live than die.
It is no task for suns to shine.
It is poor soil where some flowers will not grow.
Knowledge in youth is wisdom in age.
Knowledge is far less valuable than character.
Learn the luxury of doing good.
Learning makes a man fit company for himself.
Lost time is never found again.
Lose the day loitering—it will be the same story tomorrow, and the next more dilatory.
Manners help to make the man.
Modesty is a good virtue.
Money is a good servant, but as a master, a tyrant.
More die from too much food than too long fasting.
Nature is the beginning of everything.
No man can be true to his country who is not true to himself.
One never loses anything by being polite.
One touch of nature makes the whole world kin.
Opportunities do not await our convenience.

—Viola Vaughn[67]

The cow that you help out of the bag will be the one to hook you.
If you want to keep friends long, keep them out of your money.

—Charles Fleming[68]

LITTLE HARRY'S REPLY

It is not too common an occurrence to see whites and Negroes living next door to each other in Northern cities, and it is almost an unheard of condition in the South. Nevertheless, that is exactly what one finds in Orangeburg, South Carolina. In the western section of that city near the Edisto River, on Seaboard and Bull Streets, one finds many instances where white families live next door to Negro families, and from all reports they live in this manner without having trouble of any kind. The fact of it is the little white and colored boys often play ball together, and each side or team consists of little boys of both racial groups.

Two of these boys were great friends. The little colored boy was named Harry and the little white boy was named Lloyd. Harry and Lloyd were such good friends that they walked to school together each morning and Lloyd waited for Harry's school to turn out every afternoon so they could walk home together in the afternoons. They were many things that the little boys talked about, but neither of them ever said anything that would hurt the other's feelings.

One afternoon, however, when they were on their way home from school, Harry was surprised to hear Lloyd say, "Harry, God loved us better than He did y'all because He made us white."

"No, that ain't right," replied Harry. "He loved us better because he took time to color us!"

—William L. Davis[69]

SISTER ROSIE CHANGES HER MIND

The new preacher had just come to the little Baptist Church at Bishopville, South Carolina, and was having a meeting with the sisters of the church to see if they couldn't think of some plan to get rid of the large church debt that the preacher who preceded him had left on the church.

Among the faithful sisters of the church was Sister Rosie Wright, who had always been known as a great church worker. Sister Rosie's husband had died about a year before the new preacher had come to the church, so she was not able to give nearly as much as she was giving when her husband was living. He did not leave her any insurance money at all, and she had been forced to pay off a large funeral bill after his death. It took all the money she could rake and scrape to buy food and clothing for herself. She had to keep up the payments on the little four-room house she was buying, too.

So it was a little embarrassing to Sister Rosie to sit there in the meeting and hear the other sisters get up and say what they would give in order to pay off the church debt, when she was unable to do anything herself. She sat and listened patiently to the others, however, and when all of them had finished stating how much they would give in the church's indebtedness, Sister Rosie arose slowly and said, "I don't have nothing to give, Reverend, but if I had $1,000, I sure would give it to the church."

About two weeks later, Sister Rosie's house caught on fire and burned down. She had it insured and in less than two week's time, the fire insurance company had paid her $1,000. The preacher heard about it and went to see Sister Rosie.

"Sister Rosie," he said, "I hear you got $1,000 insurance on your house. Now you can give me that $1,000 you said you was gonna give to the church."

"Well Reverend I tell you," replied Sister Rosie, "when I was telling you about it, I had the will but I didn't have the money, and now I have the money but ain't got the will!"

—Emma Lloyd[70]

JOSHUA AND THE MOONSHINE

While Joshua was busy making moonshine, the sheriff and his deputies came up and arrested him. They carried him into Greenville and ushered him into the courthouse before the judge. The judge, after finding out what the charge against him was, said, "So you're the Joshua who made the sun stand still I guess."

"No, sir, boss," replied Joshua. "You got me sort of mixed up. I'm the Joshua that made the moon shine!"

—Genora Gray[71]

AUNT HATTIE TALKS TO GOD

One Sunday, the preacher delivered a sermon that Aunt Hattie thought she could use to help her get well. The text was: "For God sent his only beloved son in the world that whosoever believeth in Him shall not perish, but have everlasting life." "Now," thought Aunt Hattie after listening to the sermon, "here is something that I can use to cure my sickness." So Aunt Hattie went home after the church services that night, took her Bible off the table, and read the passage of scripture from which the pastor had taken his text. She read it over and over again, but it seemed as if she couldn't get the meaning of the sermon clearly fixed in her mind. She finally stopped reading and got down on her knees to say her prayers. "Oh God, please come to my relief! But don't you send your son Jesus because this ain't no time for children!"

—Rebecca Fludd[72]

TIM AND BILL FROM SUMMERVILLE

Author's note: I can personally vouch for some of the validity to this tale. While the story itself satirizes the absurdity of racial segregation, the multiracial "Brass Ankles" of the South Carolina Lowcountry really do exist. In 1982, my high school played against a high school in Walterboro, South Carolina, in Colleton County, not far from Summerville, and the number of Black girls with blonde hair and blue eyes amazed us. When I returned home that evening and I mentioned this to my mother, she explained, "Oh, those were the Brass Ankles. They're common in those parts." The "white school" referenced in the story was Summerville High School, and the "Black school" in question was Alston High School.

Summerville, South Carolina, is the home of a strange group of people of American Indian descent who vary greatly in their physical characteristics, from pale white with blue eyes to dark brown with hair of negriod texture. These people are called "Brass Ankles." No one knows their origin, but they consider themselves the equals of whites in the communities in which they live.

In Summerville and the vicinity, they are accorded all the rights and privileges granted the whites, except in a few instances. White barbers will not cut their hair in their shops, and the city operates a separate school for the Brass Ankles that goes as high as the seventh grade. White teachers teach this school and very seldom, if ever, do the Brass Ankles go to high school. All of the Brass Ankle children, regardless of the color of their skin, attend this elementary school that the city had provided for them. After they finish the sixth grade at this school, they are permitted to enroll in the White or the Negro school. Usually those who can pass for White attend the white school, and those of darker complexion attend the Negro high school.

Once there was two Brass Ankle brothers by the name of Tim and Bill. Both were in the same grade, and both finished the Brass Ankle elementary school the same year. One was white and the other was brown.

When the school term opened the next September, the boys were sent by their parents to enroll in high school. Tim, the light boy with the blue eyes, enrolled in the white high school, and his brother Bill with the copper-colored skin enrolled in the Negro high school.

The teachers at the Negro high school did not know that Bill had a brother attending a white school until the day he came to enroll in his second year. Bill struck a boy that day and was told by the principal to remain after school.

"But I can't," Bill replied. "I got to go uptown and meet my brother. He gets his books up to the white school!"

—Mr. C.S. McIver[73]

THE NEGRO CONGRESSMAN'S ANSWER
TO BEN TILLMAN

Beginning immediately after emancipation and lasting in most Southern states until 1895 was the period in United States history known as the Reconstruction period. During this time, the Negro slaves that has been freed and given the rights of citizenship, including the right to vote and hold public office, became members of the state and national law making bodies, the state legislatures and national Congress and the constitutional conventions of the various Southern states. Many of these Negroes who served as senators and representatives were well educated and extraordinary students of law. They were also very courageous and fluent speakers.

Among the Negroes in the state of South Carolina who served in the state and national legislatures was a fearless Negro politician and leader from Charleston. He served in the national Congress, but this story contains an important incident in his legislative career in South Carolina. The occasion was the session of the Constitutional Convention of 1895, at which time Ben Tillman, a white member of the convention who did not like Negroes and wanted to disfranchise them made some slighting remarks about the Negro during his absence. The Negro in turn made some uncomplimentary remarks during Tillman's absence.

Someone told Mr. Tillman what the Negro had said. The next morning, when the convention opened, Mr. Tillman arose, got the floor, and proceeded to denounce the Negro in vile terms. He became so angry that he was shaking with fury. He lost his temper entirely and shouted, "Why you dirty Black rascal, I'll swallow you alive."

"And yes," replied the Negro congressman, stamping his foot and pointing his finger in the face of Ben Tillman, "If you do, you'll have more brains in your belly than you do in your head!"

—Murray Holiday, Orangeburg County, October 17, 1944[74]

8

Tales from the Elders

During my youth, I had the honor of enjoying the tales of the last generation who grew up in the days before television, when they would educate and entertain each other by telling folk tales. My parents and other relatives and elders were amused and flattered that I enjoyed hearing their stories, not knowing that one day I would preserve them on paper. In 1991, I wrote an essay titled "The Anecdotes of Abraham Fordham" after visiting his grave on the seventh anniversary of his death. I have included that essay here along with the tales of my mother and other relatives and elders.

THE ANECDOTES OF ABRAHAM FORDHAM JR.: THE STORIES MY DAD TOLD ME IN MY YOUTH

Elephant Story

Over on Coleman Boulevard [in Mount Pleasant, South Carolina] where Channel 2's studios were, they bought old Suzy Q, an elephant, from a circus and kept her around as a gimmick to get people to watch the station. Kids would come out there and ride her and get their pictures took with her. Every now and then, she'd cause traffic jams of people lined up in their cars to stop and look at her, and one time, all that noise and horns blowing worked on the poor elephant's nerves. Old Suzy Q started roaring [imitated an elephant's roar], and she broke loose from the station and started stomping around the gas station across the street. Didn't anybody get hurt that time, but old Suzy Q. had to go after that.

Uncle Shorty and James Brown

One time when your Uncle Shorty was in the merchant marines, he went to his officer and was crying hard, letting him know that his grandmother died and had to go home on leave. He went on leave all right. He heard the singer James Brown was in town and sniffed some onions from the cook so he could cry nice and hard to get off the ship and see the show.

The Greedy Hog

Your Uncle Till had a little hog once. The hog was little but greedy. So one time, the family had a big dinner with a whole lot left over, and he fed it to the hogs. All the other hogs were fast asleep, except that one little greedy hog. When he got up the next day, don't you know Uncle Till said that little hog was so greedy, he ate 'til his little stomach had bust wide open! That's why it doesn't pay to be greedy when you eat.

The Pump and the Teeth

I lost one of my teeth when I was a little boy. Your grandmother told me to go out and pump some water for her from the old pump in the backyard. So I went out there with a bucket and started pumping. Then your grandma called me for something else, "Little Abe, LITTLE ABE!" So I turned around and let go of the pump and it went *WHACK*! My mouth was open, and that's how I lost my tooth.

The Night Before Christmas

I saw the funniest cartoon I ever saw after the war. See, they showed this man's house full of presents at Christmastime, and this voice in the background said,

'Twas the night before Christmas
And all through the house
Not a creature was stirring,
Not even a mouse.

Then this little rat pops his head out of a rat hole in the wall and says to the audience, "That's what you think!"

Cousin Charlie

Cousin Charlie was from way back in the country, way back in Awendaw, South Carolina. This boy went to see me and my first wife back in the late '50s. Now he was so far back in the woods that he ain't never been in a house with electricity before, and he was so dumb that when he was in the living room, he started screaming, "AAAAAAHHH! Abe! Abe! Come here quick."

We ran into the room, and I said, "What's the matter, Charlie?" The fool boy was sweating like a hog, and his eyes was popping out like golf balls. He said, "Somebody 'bout to shoot somebody in here!"

Don't you know that joker was looking at one of them shoot 'em up cowboy shows on TV?

The Singer at Charleston County Hall

I was at a show at County Hall once, and a fellow came out on stage that swore that he was hot stuff. He had this big guitar and called himself playing it but was really just banging on that thing. [Dad stood up and imitated the man playing the instrument to make his point.] That fellow started making all this noise that went *chang iddle lang a chang a chang chang chick a chang iddle langa chang a chang chang*, and the fool was so loud that all you could see was his mouth going up and down like he was trying to sing. [Dad then imitated the man miming to the guitar, much to my delight.] Who could hear him with all that *chang iddle lang* going on that guitar?"

117

Favorite Song

My favorite song was a little thing by Nat King Cole called "Straighten Up and Fly Right." It was a funny little tune about a buzzard taking this monkey somewhere by flying him. But while the monkey was on that buzzard's back, he started flying real crazy, going up and down and all around and the poor monkey was hanging on for dear life. See, he planned to drop the monkey and have him for dinner. But that monkey was smart! He grabbed that buzzard by the neck and told him, "Hey! Straighten up and fly right!"

Gators in the Swamp

One time my mama cooked a pot of steamed chicken for Sister Susie, who lived down by the swamp not too far from us. Miss Susie was kind of old and sick, so my mama occasionally cooked for her. So my mama said, "Abe, you take this chicken to Sister Susie Mae without fail, you hear?"

I said, "Yes, mama," and started to walk with the pot of steamed chicken. But as I started going down that road, that chicken smelled so good and my belly started growling, and before I knew it, I was sitting on a log eating the last of that chicken. So you see, I thought I was slick. I wiped all the chicken grease off my mouth and told mama that I was walking by Miss Susie's house near the swamps where the Jenkins Projects are nowadays. Anyway, I told my mama that I would have delivered the chicken, but a big fat gator crawled up out of the swamp and opened his big fat mouth and looked like he wanted to do the same thing to me that I wanted to do with the chicken, so I ran back home. There were gators in those swamps back there and then, so I guess she believed me. She fixed up another pot and told me to deliver it without fail!

So I went back down to that swamp nearby to Miss Susie's house, when all of a sudden, I saw something moving around in that muddy water. Don't you know that these beady little eyes started poking out that water and then come this big mouth looking like a trapdoor and there it was—a real live alligator!

So when that gator came up out of that swamp, I started running like a crazy man and dropped that chicken on the ground. I came back to mama all huffing and puffing out of breath and she said, "Boy, what happened to that chicken this time?" I told her the truth and she said, "Fool me once, shame on you, fool me twice, shame on me!" She grabbed a switch from the bush outside and beat my behind—*BAM, BAM, BAM*!

That's why you should never try to tell lies to grown people. They'll find out sooner or later.

Jackie and Joe

You see son, Joe Louis grew up down in Alabama, where things were really rough, and the family had to pick cotton.

They moved to Detroit, and at first, they made Joe take violin lessons. The kids laughed at him and called him a sissy for that, but then he tried something else. He took boxing lessons, and Joe soon became the best boxer around. He was soon in line to be the heavyweight champ. But then something happened.

At that time, the United States was about to go to war with Germany. You've heard about Adolf Hitler in school, right?

Hitler was ruling Germany at the time, and he had a boxer named Max Schmeling. Max was the best boxer they had in Germany, and Joe Louis was the best one here in America. But since Joe was Black, Hitler felt that Max could easily beat him.

Then in 1936, Joe Louis was on his way to being the heavyweight champ when he fought Schmeling. It was a rough fight, and Schmeling beat Joe in the twelfth round. The Black people in America were all sad over that, because in those rough days, Joe was the only champ we had. To make matters worse, Hitler was running around saying that this fight showed how weak and stupid Black people were.

Well, all that made Joe mad. Joe didn't waste time moping around and going "oh poor, poor me" like some people do. He took his lemons and made some lemonade out of them. In other words, he took a bad situation and made it good. He took all that anger inside of him over that defeat and used it to train harder and harder. First, he beat a fellow named James Braddock to become the heavyweight champ himself a year later. Then the next year, he fought Max Schmeling again.

That was really something, boy. Everybody was seated next to a radio or gathered around places that had radios to hear the fight. Joe met Max at Yankee Stadium up in New York and we all prayed that Joe would win. The announcer announced the fighters, the bell rang and *BAM*!

Joe took out all that anger and those terrible things Hitler said about himself and Black people into that fight. Mr. Potts waved his arms like a boxer as he exclaimed, "He whopped and chopped Schmeling *so* bad, that in *two minutes,* Joe Louis had Schmeling knocked out *cold*!"

I tell you it was like a Negro holiday. Black folks all over America danced in the streets because those were rough times for us, and like I said earlier, Joe Louis was the only champ we had in those days! Martin Luther King was just a little boy then. The Jews were happy, too, because of how the Germans treated them back then. Funny thing though, Joe and Max later became really good friends.

Jackie Robinson, on the other hand, was a real smart fellow who went to college, served in the army and played with the Negro Leagues. Then a white man named Branch Rickey owned the Brooklyn Dodgers, which was in the major leagues, and decided it was time to have a Black man playing for him. But he couldn't have just any old ballplayer. He had to be real smart to understand that if he fought back against some real prejudiced people, it would cause a riot in those days.

So he tried out Jackie for his Montreal team up in Canada in 1946. Jackie did really good up there, and in 1947, he brought Jackie down to Brooklyn. That was dangerous.

At first, his own teammates in Brooklyn didn't want to play with him. Branch Rickey told them he would throw them off the team. Then when he did play, other teams treated Jackie so rough that his white teammates said, "That's enough!" And since they saw that Jackie was a smart and good man, they stuck up for him.

Yeah, they gave him a rough way to go. One time they even threw a black cat on the field and said, "Look Jackie, here's your cousin." All he did was pick up the cat and stroke it. But you know, Jackie put all that anger over all this into being such a good player that he made rookie of the year for 1947 and made it possible for Black people to play in the major leagues. He also showed how good and smart we could be to the whole world, too. That meant a lot in those days.

You see, son, these fellows took out their anger in life in constructive ways that made things better instead of making them worse. Remember that when you get mad in the future.

College Song

My college days were interesting. I used to take the train from Charleston to South Carolina State in Orangeburg, and I used to work both in the laundry and the dining hall to make money to go to school. The dining hall was called Floyd Hall, and we used to sing this song about that place that went,

> *Floyd Hall Boys are we*
> *We're just as happy as we can be*
> *Oh those biscuits in the oven*
> *How I wish I had some of 'em*
> *Floyd Hall Boys are we!*

War Stories

During the war [World War II], they sent me down Fort Stewart in Georgia—right outside of Savannah in a place called Hinesville. Of course, back then, you had separate regiments of white and colored troops, just like with everything else. So we went into this mess hall, which is what they call a cafeteria in the army, and the white cook wouldn't serve us. So our major tells the cook, "Hey, you serve the colored troops just like you serve the white ones."

The fellow said, "Oh, all right. I'll serve them." And we got some scrambled eggs. But don't you know that when we started eating them eggs, we all looked at each other and noted, "You know, these are the *crunchiest* eggs I ever ate." Turns out that the cook cooked the shells in with the eggs!

So the major ran up to the cook and said, "I told you to serve these men!" That dirty cook had a little grin on his face and told the major, "Yes, sir, but you didn't say how!"

After that, they shipped us out to some place up in Iowa. We were stationed near this small town, and one night, we were allowed to go off the base. So there we were out with our uniforms in the middle of nowhere where they probably never saw nothing black but shoe polish. So we saw this guy sweeping in front of his store and decided to go there to get something to eat. A little skinny old fellow with big, thick glasses. Wouldn't you know that when he saw us coming, he got so scared that he dropped his broom, ran in the store and locked it tight!

So from there we were shipped out to Saipan, off the coast of Japan, to fight the Japanese. Boy, the Japanese weren't playing when it comes to war!

They used to do this thing called the water torture. That was where they'd tie you to the ground and slowly drop drops of water on your head. I don't know why, but after a few hours of that, it'd drive you crazy and make you feel like they were dropping hammers on your head.

But you know, one thing the Japanese troops wouldn't do to us. You see, some of the Japanese soldiers out there in the South Pacific would actually eat the white soldiers when they killed them. But they wouldn't do that to us. See, the Japanese, like a lot of people in those days, were also brainwashed into believing that we weren't as good as the whites. So that was one time I could truly say, "Thank God for prejudice!"

War is enough to drive anybody crazy, though. One night I wanted to ask my sergeant something and for no reason, he looked up and threw a knife at me. Good thing I knew how to duck his aim! I tell you, I wondered how I was going to get out of that place alive! But a few months later, I was playing a game of tennis on a makeshift court that we made, and they told us that the war was over and we'd be shipping out soon! I tell you, I got down on my knees and said, "I know I'm going to heaven because I just came back from hell! Praise God from whom all blessings flow!" So as soon as my ship came back into the port over in Charleston, I took the bus back over here and my family was so glad to see me, and I was so glad to see them.

A Tale of Revenge

Once Dad and I were taking a walk, and he showed me this mansion-like house. "Know who used to live there?" he asked.

I responded in the negative.

"That was where the mayor used to live. Many years ago, they were about to hang this Black fellow that was falsely accused of a crime. His mama came and begged the mayor to save her son's life, and the mayor said, 'Look here, this is a white man's town.'

"The mama looked at the mayor and said, 'The day is going to come where you ain't going to see nothing but Black!'

"She was right. He went blind for the rest of his life."

Beezy and the Gorilla

Back then, they used to have this carnival that came to town. They had a bunch of them before television was invented and people stopped going to things like that. They had Shuffling Sam from Alabam, Silas Green from New Orleans, a whole lot of them. Anyway, they had a tent full of these acts over where the fire station was across from where I grew up on Royall Avenue.

Yeah, they used to come once or twice a year, and people would come from miles around to see them. They had blues singers, dancers, magicians. The country people were afraid of the magicians because a lot of them were on the superstitious side. When the magicians would act like they were sawing people in half, the country folks would run! [The family enjoyed a good laugh on that note.]

They also had black-faced minstrels. These were white or colored men who dressed up with black face makeup with big red lips and do a clown show. They'd sing and tell fool stories. I remember one fellow who said his wife was so snaggle-toothed that when she opened her mouth, if her face turned sideways, it looked like the letter "K."

Then there was the gorilla wrasslin' contest. In these educated times, y'all call it wrestling, but back then, we called it wrasslin. They'd have this big ape from the zoo out there and give twenty-five dollars to anybody who would get up and wrassle him. Anyway, you know Old Blind Beezy? He lost his sight at the carnival one year. Now Old Beezy had a good job, but hearing that he could get twenty-five dollars from this, which was really good money in those days, got him greedy. So when the carnival man called for volunteers to fight the gorilla, Beezy volunteered, since he thought he could fight, but don't you know that gorilla boxed him hard in the wrong part of his head and made him blind for the rest of his life?

So while there's nothing wrong with wanting money, you have to be ever so careful of what you'll do to get some.

The Boys and the Firecrackers

I remember a few years back, up in the North Area [a local nickname for North Charleston], there was this group of boys led by this one bigger boy who thought he was a real wise guy just because he was just a little older than them—not much, but just a little. There was a supermarket up there that sold firecrackers. Anyway, the older boy got a job sweeping up the store at night, so he decided to show off for the other boys. One night he took the key the man gave him to come in and sweep up the place, and this fool let the other boys in. So he turned on the light and all the other little boys were amazed at all the firecrackers they had right in front of them, and he decided to show off some more.

The older boy thought he was big and bad now, so he wanted to show off. He said, "Y'all fellows watch this," and he took a huge Roman candle. Now you know that Roman candles aren't like regular firecrackers. They shoot up in the air and sparkle in all those pretty designs and most little boys in those days couldn't afford them. But our friend was so silly he wanted to impress the other boys by opening a window and shooting the Roman candle when he really didn't know how to, so he did. He was so ready to show off how he knew how to shoot those things that instead of putting on the ground and leaning it upward, he held it in his hand after he lit it and didn't aim the thing right. So when the Roman candle shot off, it didn't go out the window but hit a bunch of other firecrackers against the wall and pretty soon, that caused a big fire with all those explosions. The boys tried to run, but the fire was next to the doorway, and they couldn't do anything but huddle up against the wall as the fire came closer and closer to them, and the ceiling fell on them after the fire and all those explosions.

There are two morals to that story. Number one, being older doesn't always make you wiser. Second, you have to learn before you can teach.[75]

THE ANECDOTES OF PEARL MAXWELL FORDHAM: THE STORIES MY MOM TOLD ME IN MY YOUTH

Preaching and Plowing

Anyway, this fellow was plowing the field and was wiping his head because it was so hot, and the work was so hard. The fool looked up in the sky and started jumping around like he swear he got religion. "Hallelujah! Praise the Lord!" he started screaming until this old preacher from back in slavery time that they used to call the Prophet came by to see what the hollering was about.

The fellow was still screaming and jumping around like he ate some Mexican jumping beans when the Prophet asked what was wrong with him. The fool says, "I is washed with the blood and I is seen the light! I was plowing on this hot and heavy plow when I looked up there in the sky and saw these big letters up there saying 'GAP!' I know that can't mean nothing but 'go and preach,' so I'm gonna quit plowing behind this mule and do just that!'"

The old Prophet looked up in the sky, and sure enough, he saw the three letters up there, but he shook his wrinkled head and turned to the fellow and said, "Fool, that don't say 'go and preach,' it say, 'go and plow'!"

Scape Death

Scape Death was this fellow who lived in the Snowden section of Christ Church Parish who everyone thought was dead. They didn't embalm people back then and nobody knew about comas, so they had in in the church with his casket open. While the funeral was going on, Scape Death just happened to wake up from the coma and started looking around. Man, those folks started running out the church and jumping out the window like somebody threw a bomb in there! That's why they called him Scape Death, because he escaped death!

Evil Spirits

One night when you were about a year old [1965–66], we left you with your grandmother, and as we were coming down the block to pick up the child, we heard you screaming to the top of your little lungs. We rushed inside and saw you in the crib with a red ribbon tied so tight around your fat little legs that your circulation was cut off. Your grandma said, "Child, this baby been making so much noise I had to use this ribbon to get the evil spirits off of him."

I told your grandma, "Janie, get that mess off my boy's leg right now!"

The Hell No Sermon

Up at Olive Branch AME over in Christ Church Parish, we had a Reverend W.T. Murray, who used to preach what he liked to call the "Hell No Sermon." He'd ask the congregation, "Do you want to go to hell?" And they'd all say, "No!"

Anatomy Lesson

They tried to teach anatomy at the little schoolhouse I went to, but the children's minds were so low and they said such nasty things about the body parts that they had to take anatomy out of the school.

ANECDOTES AND FOLK TALES OF OTHER ELDERS

Boy, you better not make noise or act up when 'e lightning and thundering. That's God talking when it does that. One time your granddaddy was smoking a pipe and reading the paper while it was thundering and lightening, and I said, "Abe, you better mind! The Lord don't like that!" Sure enough, lightening came through the house and cut your granddaddy's pipe in half while he was still sitting in the chair. You'll bet he never smoked that pipe while it was lightening and thundering no more!

—told to the author by Janie Fordham,
the author's grandmother, in the 1970s

Oh yeah, y'all know how nowadays they got them big iron trains that makes all this noise and smoke when they takes folks from place to place. Well, one day this gal from the country took a train trip up north for the first time so she can mind her sister's children. Well, the colored gal fell asleep, and the train then gone into a tunnel. That little gal woke up when the train was good and dark in the tunnel and said, "Great God, the buckra [white man] done run us in the ground!"

—Story heard at Friendship AME Church in
Mount Pleasant, South Carolina, in the 1970s

There was this one fellow who was making some cheap, bootleg whiskey called "Fight Your Mama." Anyway, somebody told the police chief on him. So the chief of police went out there, and the fool was not only making that junk, he was drinking it, too. So naturally, he didn't have the sense to run away or try to hide what he was doing from the cop. To make matters worse, that fool boy actually offered the chief some of the Fight Your Mama whiskey. Needless to say, they carried his dumb behind right off to jail.

—story told to the author by Douglas Richardson of Mount Pleasant, South Carolina, in the 1980s

Yeah, there was a country fellow that I knew from one of those Sea Islands near Charleston. [He] was one of what you call those kleptomaniacs, always bothering other people's stuff, including their medicine. I swear he couldn't leave other people's things alone to save his life. Well anyway, I had to go to the army doctor because I had a kidney infection, and the pills they gave me caused my urine to change color. So I had an idea to fix that thieving country boy.

Well, I left one of those pills on my bunk next to some junk that I had in my pockets that I didn't care about, and sure enough, I hid and saw that country boy take my stuff. I had some mints mixed in with the pill, so he swallowed the mints along with the pill. Then I jumped up and yelled, "Gotcha!" Since I caught him red-handed, he started stammering and apologizing, and I said, "Oh no, it's too late now!" I took these chicken bones I saved from the mess hall and put them on the ground. I started flapping my arms and doing this crazy dance and yelled, "Wings of bone and head of gerbil, very soon you will pee purple.'"

I knew that would scare him because I heard him talk about believing in roots and spells and stuff like that. So the next morning, we were at the latrine and sure enough, the country boy went to use the bathroom and he looked down and screamed like a woman seeing a rat! He ran over to me while he ran over to me and yelled, "Alright Charles, just take the spell off of me. I ain't gonna steal nobody's stuff no more."

—story told to the author by Charles Brown, Mount Pleasant, South Carolina, in the early 2000s

I used to be the cook for those white children at Moultrie High School [in Mount Pleasant, South Carolina]. The time came when I wanted to quit, so I just stopped going. Not too long after that, the white children came over to my place and said, "Marie, please come back. They ain't serving us nothing but slop since you left." So I went back, and they paid me more money.

—story told to the author by Marie "May" Brown,
Mount Pleasant, South Carolina, in the 1970s

I'd go over on South Liberty Street, where most of the Black folks in Spartanburg did their business. There was this building at 371 South Liberty Street that housed Mr. Joe Patton's barbershop and a Negro clinic run by Dr. John C. Bull, a light-skinned, heavyset man who you never saw without a cigarette in his mouth. Now as such, he was a pretty respected fellow in town, and the Blacks were always coming up to him to borrow money.

He was a busy fellow, being the doctor for the Negro neighborhoods, so sometimes he'd go outside of the clinic and sit down in his chair and go to sleep. But you want to know something? People would walk up to him while he was asleep and put the money they owned him in his pockets, so he would always wake up with his pockets full of money from the people he trusted and cared about to lend it to them.

That's why it pays to do good. Sometimes it comes back to you.

—story told to the author by Mr. Joseph Kimpson (who taught at Carver
High School in Spartanburg in the 1950s and 1960s)
during the late 1980s

Before I taught in Spartanburg, I went to Benedict College in Columbia, South Carolina. I started seeing this pretty girl who, if you didn't know better, you would think was white. One day we went on a date at the Carolina Theater on Main Street, and some white men saw me with her and beat me up in the middle of the street. Of course, there was no use calling the police for something like that in those days. It was things like that that made me determined to get and education and work to change things from the inside so your generation wouldn't have to go through such things.

—story told to the author by Mr. Joseph Kimpson in
Columbia, South Carolina, in the late 1980s

I played football for Carver High, the Black high school in Spartanburg in the early '60s. Spartanburg High was the white high school, and we used to wonder if we could beat them or not. So one day, we took a chance and went to Spartanburg High's field and said we wanted to have a scrimmage with them. They said sure, and we started playing against each other. All was fine and good until one of their coaches came on the field and said, "What the hell are y'all niggers doing here?" The white kids were about to explain that it was OK with them until the coach said, "Aw hell no," and put his pistol in the air and fired. Needless to say, we didn't stick around to argue.

—story told to the author by Reuben Reeder,
Spartanburg, South Carolina, in the early 1990s

I was one of the first Black policemen in Spartanburg back in the early 1960s, and I was often asked to serve as a bodyguard for Senator Strom Thurmond. One time I was guarding him when he was talking all kinds of mess about Black people and civil rights to a crowd of white folks, but when he was around Black people, he was nice as he could be. One day, I asked him if he really believed all that junk he said against Black people and civil rights, and he said, "Sam, when y'all colored people start voting in large numbers, I won't talk like that no more."

—story told to the author by Samuel McGowan,
Spartanburg, South Carolina, 1999

I went to the Avery Institute here in Charleston back in the 1930s. It was something. I used to be good at spelling, and one day, the principal, Mr. Benjamin Cox, had a spelling contest. I looked forward to it because I would get my first pair of long pants if I won, and that made you a man back then. Anyhow, the day of the spelling bee came, and when they asked me to spell *cheese*, I said, "C-H-E-E-S." So when we went home that night, I wanted some macaroni and cheese with my dinner, and mama said, "You can't spell it, so you can't eat it!"

So needless to say, I couldn't get the long pants, so no gal in Charleston would be seen with me then. I had to go out with them gals in the country!

—story told to the author by John Carr,
Charleston, South Carolina, in the 1990s

They had this comedian at the Apollo Theater in Harlem. They called him Stepin Fetchit. I think his real name was Lincoln Perry or something like that. Step was supposed to be the laziest man on Earth, and one night, he came on the stage with a wheelbarrow turned upside down. Another fellow on stage asked, "Step, why is that wheelbarrow upside down?" And Step answered in his lazy, draggy voice, "If I had it right-side up, somebody might put something in it!"

—story told to the author by Jimmy Scott,
Mount Pleasant, South Carolina, circa 1978

Now at this time, my friends of mine, I'm playing a sound from underground
    to move and groove you
Fixed up in shimmy style and if you wanna shimmy awhile, stick around,
    don't be no clown honey child
You must be pleased Louise as I put your mind at ease with sounds like these!

—rhyme by "Honest" John Pembroke of Honest John's Record Store in
Charleston, South Carolina, circa 1961
(A precursor to rap music, Mr. Pembroke's shouted rhymes of this kind
    played on a loudspeaker from his record store to attract customers.)

Then there was that preacher that had that church over in West Ashley that used to be on the radio. Back when the gals were walking around showing their big fine legs in those short dresses, he got up on one sermon and said, "I say the women these days, they wear the skirts so high up on they legs, that when they bend over, you can see they chittlings!"

—story told by Lee Brown in the 1970s

When my sister was a little girl, she and our Aunt Effie Rochell were at one of the stores in downtown Spartanburg, and she had to go to the bathroom.
    "Where is the bathroom?" asked Aunt Effie. "My niece has to go."
    The nasty shop owner said, "We don't let colored people use the bathroom here."
    Aunt Effie replied, "OK then, bring out a mop and bucket."
    "Why?" asked the shop owner.

Aunt Effie responded, "So since she can't use your bathroom, she can do it out here on the bucket, and you can clean it up if it spills."

They let her use the bathroom.

Sweet Daddy Grace was a preacher back then who had a long white beard and long hair down to his shoulders and used to have all these parades where they would baptize people in the street with fire hoses.

Me and Anne heard the Sweet Daddy Grace followers playing their trombones and drums and dancing in the streets outside their church over on Highland Avenue. Sweet Daddy Grace was walking around with his big hat and long hair down to his shoulders and fancy suit while these two pretty girls were fanning him when he walked like he was something out of ancient Egypt. So we went to hear Sweet Daddy Grace out of curiosity, and those people were going wild with their tambourines, jumping up and down, and beating on washboards while the preacher was screaming at the top of his lungs in the pulpit. You didn't see that kind of stuff too often outside of the country areas, so then we started to laugh. The ushers got angry and started coming toward us, and we ran out of the church. Your granddaddy Jesse Montgomery was driving by in his taxicab and stopped and asked us what was wrong. We told him, and Daddy said, "That's what y'all get for making fun of other people's church."

—both Stories told by Barbara Montgomery Collier,
Spartanburg, South Carolina, 2016

One time when I was in church, the preacher was preaching, and this fellow got up with a wild look on his face with something under his arm. While the preacher kept preaching, the fellow walked up to the pulpit and help up an Earth, Wind, and Fire album and said, "This album is god!"

The ushers tackled him and dragged him off the pulpit.

—story told by Louis Reid, 1986

The next time you see that fool over there, you call him the Disco Hog.

Why is that?

We had a party at my house, and while everybody's dancing, all he want to do was eat! This fool gone in the kitchen and went straight to the pots on the stove. He took off the lids and looked in the pots while my mama was cooking, and she told him to get lost. Next time you see him, call him the Disco Hog!

—overheard by the author while he was a student at
Wando High School, Mount Pleasant, South Carolina, 1979

Your grandfather Jesse Montgomery was also my uncle. He used to drive cabs with me for the DeLuxe Cab Company here in Spartanburg. One time back in either the late '50s or early '60s, I went with him to one of the local banks, and [he] had his usual scowl on his face. One of the white ladies who worked at the bank said, "Why don't you smile?" Uncle Jesse looked at the lady and said, "I ain't got a damn thing to smile about!" That took guts in those days.

—story told to the author by Charles Atchison Sr.,
Spartanburg, South Carolina, December 2016

We were coming home from a party late one night and we were rushing to get home because it was almost past our curfew. As we were speeding back, we were about to rush across the train tracks, and it just so happened that we were in such a hurry that we barely missed getting hit by the train. That's when I realized that while rules are rules, it's sometimes better to break them and stay alive.

—story told to the author by Patricia Montgomery McDonald,
Spartanburg, South Carolina, 2000

One time I went to hear this sermon over in Salem Baptist Church in downtown Charleston, and there was this old man there in his best Sunday suit, writing down everything the preacher was saying with his pencil stub in a composition book. That fellow looked really serious about what he was doing, but when I passed by him to use the bathroom, I noticed that all he was doing was writing a bunch of chicken scratch and scribble scrabble that didn't make a piece of sense. I later learned that that poor old fellow was a shoeshine man that couldn't read or write. All day long, he dealt with people treating him like he was dirt. The white folks were calling him names while he was trying to make a few cents if he didn't shine their shoes just right. So once a week, he would put on the only suit he had and make like he was some kind of church secretary, and it made him feel good. When people always treat you like nobody, you'll do what you can to feel like somebody.

—story from Mr. James Campbell,
Charleston, South Carolina, around 2017

There was the family who was poor and hungry and ragged, just the mama working two jobs to feed a house full of children after her husband died. He said that one night the little boy got down on his knees and prayed that God would send the family something to eat. Don't you know that the family was living in a shack next to the train tracks, and that very night, a train with a refrigerated car full of food had a wreck by the shack and the food was scattered all over the place. The family got up and picked up as much food as they could, and the mama said, "Thank the Lord for this praying child!"

—sermon from Reverend Louis O. Johnson Sr., Olive Branch
AME Church, Mount Pleasant, South Carolina, 1970s[76]

SPARTANBURG STORIES OF
REVEREND BOOKER T. SEARS JR.

BORN IN 1939 IN COLUMBIA, SOUTH CAROLINA; PASTORED IN SPARTANBURG, SOUTH CAROLINA; AND PRESENTLY PASTORS AT GOODWILL BAPTIST CHURCH IN BRONX, NEW YORK

We moved to Anderson, South Carolina, in 1947, when I was in the third grade, and we stayed until I was in fifth grade. I was glad to get out of Anderson, because the Ku Klux threatened us at least twice a week if not more. My dad (Reverend Booker T. Sears Sr.) and a Black physician, Dr. Young, reinstated the National Association for the Advancement of Colored People (NAACP) in Anderson, so with that, we lived under the threat of annihilation, of severe bodily harm. Oftentimes, my mother had to call one of the deacons of the church when the Klan would set across from the field from where we lived, and the men of the church would come from the back of the church and have their shotguns ready. In 1949, when Daddy told us that I was going to a new school in a place called Spartanburg, all I wanted to do was get out of Anderson, where I thought I would never live to be ten years old.

555 Wofford Street, Spartanburg, South Carolina, December 1, 1949. On that day. I had my first bath in a real bathtub, instead of a no. 3 tin tub. No more toting firewood, stove wood and buckets of coal. 555 had gas heaters, and a gas cook stove. 555 Wofford in the Hamburg section of Spartanburg was our home and was often the stopping place for many well-known African Americans who came at any hour, often unannounced. We were not in the *Green Book*, but we were the Green House at 555 Wofford Street. The house is still there. You name them, the personalities would stay there. At one point, Reverend Martin Luther King's uncle Reverend Joel King was pastoring at Mt. Moriah Baptist Church in Spartanburg, and once or twice, young Dr. Martin Luther King Jr., would stop at our place to spend the night in Spartanburg while driving from Atlanta on his way to Crozier University in Pennsylvania. He was a little guy but very sharp. He was cool with his attire. This was before he was famous. I knew that there was something unusual about him, with that baritone voice. He could pitch a good game of horseshoes [laughs].

There was a superintendent; I think his name was Mr. Hallman. I was in the fifth grade at Highland School, and the superintendent made his annual visit. The teacher prepared the bulletin boards with our papers with math and pictures of Black heroes Booker T. Washington, George Washington Carver and Mary McLeod Bethune. The superintendent came into the room with his wife and the principal, and they paid no attention to the bulletin board that we spent all that time preparing. The superintendent's wife asked our teacher, "I see you have a piano. Do they know 'Dixie'?" The teacher said, "Yes, ma'am." The teacher went to the piano and told us to stand and sing "Dixie." The superintendent's wife said, "One of your students, is there something wrong with him because he's not singing?" The teacher said, "Booker T., go to the office." The principal was angry, "Why would you do this? You could have gotten this school in trouble!" So he gave me some lashes in my hands with that old leather strap and a note to take home to my parents. To add more to it because I had misbehaved, my daddy was about to get the belt on me. I told her, and my mother said, "Don't you put a lick on him!" I could not sing about "I wish I was in the land of cotton." It felt it was an insult. She didn't care about whether we could write or do math. All she wanted was for us to entertain her by singing "Dixie."

After urban renewal hit Spartanburg, I was in the post office over on South Church Street when a guy came in and said, "Hey, do you live here?" I said, "Yeah." He said, "I've been drinking, but I know I'm not drunk. I haven't been to Spartanburg in twenty or thirty years, and I wanted to show my girlfriend the places on the Southside where I grew up. I know I've been drinking, and I couldn't find anything!" I said, "Those things are no longer there. Model Cities program and urban renewal wiped them out." Many years later, I learned that "urban renewal" meant "Negro removal" [laughs]. My old house is one of the few still standing from that era.

Near to our house was the Bethel Fire Baptized Holiness Church. It was called the "Meeting House in Dixie" back in the segregated days. The church was at 212 Pine Street, and the church used to come on the radio on Saturday night. The church was packed, and they would dance and beat the tambourines and the white people would come to the church for entertainment. The parsonage was right next door to us. I didn't have an appreciation for that church because I personally heard bishop tell the congregation during their annual conference, "Do not be bothered around Martin Luther King and voting. Y'all stay out of white folk's business!" Nobody told me that. I heard it out of my own ears. Ironically, the bishop and the King family lived two doors apart on Auburn Avenue in Atlanta!

On January 11, 1965, I walked into the South Carolina National Bank on East Main Street in Spartanburg. My title was operations officer. I wore a suit and a tie, They needed somebody, and I was handpicked, as I was fresh out of Benedict College in Columbia, South Carolina. I did not apply for it; they approached me, probably through my connections with my father and the local preachers. They would pray over me when I got the job. I studied from the American Institute of Banking and studied commercial law and commercial loans. They prepared the whites for my presence, but my back still burns to this day from those eyes staring at me. I stayed there for five years before I left to preach full time.[77]

9

The Journals of Abraham Fordham

When most people lose their parents to time, they often wish that they could remember some of the stories they told or the advice they gave. While the current generation lives in an era in which technology can record conversations with their parents in their lifetimes, those of us of a certain age did not have that privilege.

My dad, Abraham Fordham Jr., was different in that regard. He was never a famous man, but he kept diaries from his days as a college student at South Carolina State College in Orangeburg though his adventures in World War II, up to the letters he wrote to me in college shortly before his death in 1984. He saved all of these in his briefcase, which is, today, among my prized possessions. Some of these writings also provide an insight into the thoughts of a member of a bygone generation of Black South Carolinians, who rarely left such documents behind.

In 1943, while a student at South Carolina State, he expressed these thoughts about growing up amid World War II.

CHRISTMAS 1943

Guardian shepherds heard the songs of peace and sought the lowly shed where Christ was born. Where now can angels sing that war shall cease? Without such songs our lives are left forlorn. For now the skies bear argoses of wrath that shake the trembling earth and trackless sea; and modern vandals tread a flaming path to trample into dust all charity.

If we will walk with faith the Christ-like way, and build a brotherhood of worldwide scope that finds God's face in every child today; where creed nor caste destroys man's cherished hope—we shall be rid of war and racial hate, for love and justice then will rule the state.

FAITH

Two thousand years ago, he for whom Christmas is named gave us a faith equal to all the needs of humanity. Today in thousands of homes, that faith, tested through the centuries, brings hope anew. These are the homes where a vacant chair testifies the strength of that faith within the absent member: these are the homes where those remaining find faith, the dearest gift of this yuletide. Matched by courageous endeavor, that faith is leading our country to righteous victory. Now as always, the Christmas message for Americans is a message of cheer, because it is a message of great faith. God rest ye merry gentlemen, let nothing you dismay, remember Christ our savior was born on Christmas Day. To save us all from Satan's power when we were gone astray.

LET'S BRING NEW GLORY TO OLD GLORY

Let's bring new glory to Old Glory. The flag of our America, let us show the world a big parade of men that have the stuff that heroes are made of.

Let's bring new glory to Old Glory, with faith and courage, we will win through. So wave on Old Glory, and with the help of God, we'll bring new glory to you.

UNTITLED MUSINGS

I see my way as birds their trackless way.
I shall arrive! What time, what circuit first?
I ask not.
In some time, his good time, I shall arrive.
He guides me and the bird. In his good time.

The art of making love.
Don't try to love a person before you explore her to see what is there.
Be nice but have a purpose. When you find one, go after her and find what's there. And make her love you.
People marry for a complete personality. You alone only represents half of your personality. When you marry, you complete the twain with companionship and fellowship.

Whenever people get sense enough to think that religion in a way of life, and art, and a beauty, and shall train the minds of the youth in science of the art of religion. Then the church will have no fear of religion failing. The church will be a recreational center where people will go after their work to hear lectures, speeches, etc. He will go to church to be refreshed, renewed, to get his spirit lifted.

Peace cannot be made between two peoples who never forgive, neither can it be made between two peoples who are blind to one another's virtues and saturated with the hate that rises from one another's faults. And perhaps one of the most certain ways of demobilizing the war mind is to ask the great God of all men to stand guard over our souls with a flaming sword, that we may be saved from that corruption of soul which will make peace unacceptable to us when it comes. It is just here that the church of the Living God must be prepared to serve.[78]

THE AUTOBIOGRAPHY OF ABRAHAM FORDHAM

(WRITTEN CIRCA 1950)

I was born June 18, 1922, at Whilden Street in Mount Pleasant, South Carolina. I am the fourth of eighteen children. I entered Laing Elementary School at the age of seven and graduated high school at the age of eighteen. I was retained in the fourth grade one year, the only class in my education career. I delivered the salutatory oration before leaving high school, I went to South Carolina State College after leaving high school in the year 1941. I spent three joyous years and seven months at State before being called into the armed services. Taking my final exams about two months ahead of time before [being] inducted, I didn't know whether I would graduate or not. After being in the service about two and a half months, I saw my name in a Virginia newspaper as being one to receive a BS degree from South Carolina State College.

I completed my basic training where upon I was chosen as one to enter Non-Commissioned Officer Training School. During that six weeks we learned everything from keeping the grounds clean to the duties of the captain in charge of a company. I then went from one camp to another until finally I was at Camp Beale in California. From there, [I went] to Fort Lawton in Washington and then over to a small island in the Pacific, Saipan. This was where I received my acceptance papers to Meharry Medical Institution. Being surrounded by Japanese and half-afraid, I threw my papers in the trash and my opportunity to attend medical school.

I left Saipan and went to Guam, where I worked from a dentist's assistant up to Sergeant in charge of the dispensary, a position I held until I was discharged in 1945. I came home to my family and friends, and I took a job at Pirates' Cruize Gardens. I worked there for about two and a half years mowing, fertilizing, pruning and caring for plants. I then went to New York, where I worked at Commuter's Wine and Liquor for a few months. I was called home to work at Laing High School in 1950, where I now work. I like outdoor life, such as photography, fishing and hunting. I dislike making public speeches and raising money.[79]

African Epilogue

In the introduction of this book, I mentioned my adventures in West Africa and that region's connection to the storytelling culture of Black South Carolinians. The following incident would suffice to conclude this anthology.

While in Senegal, we visited a village of the Fulani people. I noticed that they kept staring at me and repeating the words, "Wolof! Wolof!" I asked our translator what they meant, and he explained, "They think you are of the Wolof people and wonder why you are speaking English and dressed like an American."

Throughout that visit, people in Senegal and Gambia would say that I was a member of the Wolof people because of my physical features. When we went to the Black Civilizations Museum in Dakar and met Khady Ba, who was discussed in this book's first chapter, we kept staring at each other because of our strong physical resemblance, and our translator smiled and introduced me to her by saying, "Professor, come meet your Wolof sister."

If this were not enough, I looked up the Wolof people online when I returned to the hotel. Part of the article contained these words: "In Wolof and Senegalese society, there are professional storytellers known as griots. They are historians, poets, musicians and entertainers."

A short time later, I visited some first cousins in Spartanburg, South Carolina, and told them of my African sojourn. One cousin, Elaisha Gibson, said, "Brace yourself for this." She showed me a DNA test she took that revealed that we were of 16 percent Wolof ancestry, along with percentages from the Igbos of Nigeria.

Thus, I learned my interest in these matters came naturally, and this was a reminder of the importance in keeping storytelling traditions alive.[80]

Notes

Preface

1. Talley, *Negro Traditions*, 151.

African Prologue

2. This chapter is a condensed version of two articles by the author, "African Stories," and "More African Stories," which appeared in the *Charleston Mercury* in September and October 2023, respectively.

1. Testimonies from the Attempted Denmark Vesey Rebellion

3. Hamilton, *Negro Plot*, 19.
4. Ibid., 36.
5. Ibid., 36–37.
6. Ibid., 37.
7. Ibid., 37–38.
8. Ibid., 42–43.
9. Ibid., 43–45.

2. Stories of Slavery

10. Interview of Bradley Gilmore by Caldwell Sims in Union, South Carolina, in *Slave Narratives: South Carolina*, 14:120–23.
11. Interview conducted by Leonarda J. Aimar in Charleston, South Carolina, on October 16, 1917, in "Stories Collected from Slaves," Agatha Simmons Collection, College of Charleston, Charleston, South Carolina.
12. Coffin, *Freedom Triumphant*, 370.
13. Interview of Thomas Goodwater by Augustus Ladson in Charleston, South Carolina, in *Slave Narratives: South Carolina*, 14:166–70.
14. Interview of Henry Brown by Augustus Ladson, in *Slave Narratives: South Carolina*, 14:222–26.
15. Interview of Susan Hamilton by Augustus Ladson, in *Slave Narratives: South Carolina*, 14:233–34.
16. Interview of Elijah Green by Augustus Ladson, in *Slave Narratives: South Carolina*, 14:195–99.
17. Interview of Daniel Goddard by Stiles Scruggs in Columbia, South Carolina, in *Slave Narratives: South Carolina*, 14:149–52.
18. Interview of Jerry Hill by F.S. DuPre in Spartanburg, South Carolina, in *Slave Narratives: South Carolina*, 14:289–90.
19. Interview of George McAlilley by W.W. Dixon in Winnsboro, South Carolina, in *Slave Narratives: South Carolina*, 14:143–45.
20. Interview of Charity Moore by W.W. Dixon in Winnsboro, South Carolina, in *Slave Narratives: South Carolina*, 14:205–7.
21. Interview of Reverend John B. Elliott by Stiles Scruggs in Columbia, South Carolina, in *Slave Narratives: South Carolina*, 14:3–5.
22. "Former Slave Tells Story of Days Before 'De War,'" *Spartanburg Herald*, November 12, 1933, 3.
23. Interview of Ann J. Edwards, in Fort Worth, Texas, in *Slave Narratives: Texas*, 16:10–14.
24. Interview with Hampton Fiedler in Columbia, South Carolina, in "Unpublished Ex-Slave Narratives."

3. Tales of the Supernatural

25. Interview of George Brown, janitor for R.E. Biber, optometrist, by F.S. Du Pre, in Spartanburg, South Carolina, on June 10, 1937.

26. Told by Mrs. S.C. Ladson, age thirty-six, maid, of 180 King Street, Charleston, South Carolina, to Augustus Ladson, South Carolina Negro Writers' Project.

27. Told by Joe C. Williams, age eighty-six, member of Mother Emanuel AME Church, to Augustus Ladson, South Carolina Negro Writers' Project.

28. Told by George Brown to Chalmers S. Murray, in *South Carolina Folk Tales*, 50–51.

29. Interview of Thomas Goodwater, in *Slave Narratives: South Carolina*, 14:169.

30. Told by Mildred Hare, in *South Carolina Folk Tales*, 47.

31. Told to Dromgoole Ham, in *South Carolina Folk Tales*, 47.

32. Told to Augustus Ladson, in *South Carolina Folk Tales*, 58–60.

33. Told by Laura L. Middleton, in *South Carolina Folk Tales*, 50.

4. Animal and Trickster Tales

34. Christensen, *Afro-American Folk Lore*, 1–5, 62–73.

35. Ibid., 84–86.

36. Ibid., 101–3.

37. Told by Maria Middleton of Corners Plantation in St. Helena Island, South Carolina in 1919, collected by Elsie Clews Parson, in *Folk Lore of the Sea Islands*, 38.

38. Told by an unidentified student at Port Royal Industrial School, in *Folk Lore of the Sea Islands*, 137.

39. Told by Henry Middleton, the husband of Maria, in *Folk Lore of the Sea Islands*, 119.

40. Told by Justine Brow, aged about sixty-five, of Spanish Ville Plantation, Hilton Head Island, South Carolina, in *Folk Lore of the Sea Islands*, 110–11.

41. Told by Laura A. Younge, a student at Port Royal and Industrial Agricultural School, in *Folk Lore of the Sea Islands*, 118.

42. Henry C. Davis, "Notes on Negro Lore," *Columbia State*, December 7, 1913, 3.

43. Collected by Chlotide R. Martin in Beaufort County, South Carolina, in *South Carolina Folk Tales*, 18.

44. *South Carolina Folk Tales*, 34.

45. Told by Henrietta Johnson, a pupil at Port Royal Industrial School, age sixteen, of Old Grey's Hill, Port Royal Island, South Carolina, in *Folk Lore of the Sea Islands*, 75.

5. Anecdotes of Black Orators

46. *Proceedings of the Constitutional Convention*, 421.
47. Cong. Rec., 43rd Cong., 1st Sess., 565–67.
48. Cong. Rec. (1875), 958–60.
49. Robert Brown Elliott, "The Civil Rights Bill: Extracts from a Speech Delivered in the House of Representatives," in *Charleston Syllabus: Readings on Race, Racism, and Racial Violence*, edited by Chad Williams, Kidada E. Williams and Keisha N. Blain (Athens: University of Georgia Press, 2016), 122. The Civil Rights Bill of 1875 that Rainey, Elliot and Cain argued for to end segregation in public places was passed in 1875, but in 1883, it was declared unconstitutional. A later version of the bill would pass in 1964.
50. Adapted from the *Charleston News and Courier*, February 23, 1948, 3.

6. Profiles and Narratives

51. James Holloway interviewed by Augustus Ladson, in "The Charleston Insurrection: Controversies of Origin and Result," South Carolina Negro Writers' Project.
52. Interview with the Honorable Thomas E. Miller by Augustus Ladson, South Carolina Negro Writers' Project. Miller died in 1938.
53. Interview of Mary H. Wright by Hattie Mobley, South Carolina Negro Writers' Project. *See also, Spartanburg Herald Journal*, January 31, 2012; and *Spartanburg Herald Journal*, August 12, 2020.
54. Caldwell, *History of the American Negro*, 291–93.
55. Interview with Mary Ray Saxon, the daughter of Celia Dial Saxon, by Lilian Buchannan, South Carolina Negro Writers' Project. In 2016, the University of South Carolina in Columbia honored Saxon by naming the Celia Dial Saxon Hall after her.
56. Original article by the author.
57. Ibid.

7. Forgotten Stories from the Archives

58. Told by Rubertha Polite, a student at Penn School, St. Helena Island, South Carolina, in *Folk Lore of the Sea Islands*, 133–34.

59. Told by Hagar Campbell, of Charleston, South Carolina, South Carolina Negro Writers' Project.

60. Interview with Queen Breech, housekeeper, thirty years of age, of 55 Kennedy Street, Charleston, South Carolina, South Carolina Negro Writers' Project.

61. Told by Victoria Attles, of 14 Porter's Court, Charleston, South Carolina, South Carolina Negro Writers' Project.

62. Told by Mrs. Irene Noisette, seamstress, about forty-five years of age, of 26 Clifford Street, Charleston, South Carolina, to Augustus Ladson, South Carolina Negro Writer's Project.

63. Henry C. Davis, "Notes on Negro Lore," *Columbia State*, December 7, 1913, 3.

64. Told by Joseph S. Shanklin, a student at Port Royal Industrial and Agricultural School, in *Folk Lore of the Sea Islands*, 52–53.

65. Told by Mr. W.S. Noisette of 26 Clifford Street, about forty-three years of age, cabinetmaker and upholsterer, to Augustus Ladson of the South Carolina Negro Writers' Project.

66. Told by Ruby Gomez, age forty-five, of 178 Spring Street, Charleston, South Carolina, to Laura Middleton of the South Carolina Negro Writer's Project.

67. Told by Viola Vaughn, age forty, 36 Rose Lane, Charleston, South Carolina, to Laura Middleton of the South Carolina Negro Writer's Project.

68. Told by Charles Fleming, age sixty-five, Mount Pleasant, South Carolina, to Laura Middleton of the South Carolina Negro Writer's Project.

69. Told by William L. Davis of Orangeburg County, South Carolina, February 19, 1945, collected by J. Mason Brewer, in *Humorous Folk Tales*, 22.

70. Told by Emma Lloyd, Marlboro County, SC, November 2, 1944, to Mattie E. Fisher, collected by J. Mason Brewer, in *Humorous Folk Tales*, 36.

71. Told by Genora Gray of Greenville County, South Carolina, on October 22, 1944, to Bessie A. Goldsmith, in *Humorous Folk Tales*, 62.

72. Told by Rebecca Fludd in Charleston County, South Carolina, on December 4, 1944, to J. Mason Brewer, in *Humorous Folk Tales*, 35.

73. Told by Mr. C.S. McIver in Dorchester County, South Carolina, on March 12, 1945, to Miss Mattie E. Mouzon, in *Humorous Folk Tales*, 21. Incidentally, years later, a relative from North Carolina told me an anecdote about a similar racially mixed and ambiguous group of people in that state called the "Issues." When I asked why they were called this, she explained, "Because people used to ask them, 'Is you white, is you Black or is you Indian?'"

74. Told by Murray Holiday in Orangeburg County, on October 17, 1944, in *Humorous Folk Tales*, 7.

8. Tales from the Elders

75. From the author's personal manuscript, "The Anecdotes of Abraham Fordham Jr.," 1991. *The Charleston News and Courier* of January 4, 1964, on page 1-B, reported a fireworks fire at a Livingston's Supermarket in North Charleston similar to the fire in my father's story.
76. These stories are from personal notebooks and recollections of the author.
77. The author's telephone interview with Reverend Booker T. Sears Jr., January 19, 2024.

9. The Journals of Abraham Fordham

78. From the journals of Abraham Fordham Jr., circa 1943 to 1952, in the author's possession.
79. The untitled autobiography of Abraham Fordham Jr., circa 1950, in the author's possession.

African Epilogue

80. Personal recollections of the author.

Selected Bibliography

Books

Adams, Edward C.L. *Tales of the Congaree*. Chapel Hill: University of North Carolina Press, 1987.

Bontemps, Arna, and Langston Hughes, ed. *The Book of Negro Folklore*. New York: Dodd, Mead, 1958.

Botkin, B.A. *A Treasury of American Folklore*. New York: Crown Publishers, 1945.

Bradford, Roark. *Ol' King David and the Philistine Boys*. New York: Harper and Brothers, 1930.

————. *Ol' Man Adam and His Chillun*. New York: Harper and Brothers, 1928.

Brewer, J. Mason, ed. *Humorous Folk Tales of the South Carolina Negro*. Orangeburg: South Carolina Negro Folklore Guild, 1945.

Caldwell, Arthur Bunyan. *History of the American Negro, South Carolina Edition*. Atlanta, GA: A.B. Caldwell Publishing Company, 1919.

Christensen, Abbie M.H. *Afro-American Folk Lore Told Round Cabin Fires on the Sea Islands of South Carolina*. Boston, MA: J.G. Cupples Company, 1892.

Coffin, Charles. *Freedom Triumphant: The Fourth Period of the War of the Rebellion from September 1864, to Its Close*. New York: Harper Brothers, 1891.

Gates, Henry Louis, and Maria Tatar, ed. *The Annotated African American Folktales*. New York: Liveright Publishing Corporation, 2018.

Gonzales, Ambrose. *The Black Border: Gullah Stories of the Carolina Coast.* Columbia, SC: The State, 1922.

Hamilton, James. *Negro Plot: An Account of the Late Intended Insurrection Among a Portion of the Blacks of the City of Charleston, South Carolina*: Boston, MA: Joseph W. Ingraham, 1822.

Hamilton, Virginia. *The People Could Fly: American Black Folktales.* New York: A.A. Knopf, 1985.

Harris, Joel Chandler. *The Complete Tales of Uncle Remus.* New York: Houghton Mifflin, 2002.

Hurston, Zora Neale. *Mules and Men.* Philadelphia, PA: J.P. Lippincott and Company, 1935.

Jones, Charles Colcock. *Gullah Folktales from the Georgia Coast.* Athens: University of Georgia Press, 2000.

Lester, Julius. *Black Folktales.* New York: Grove Press, 1970.

Niumi, Fort Bullen, and the Abolition of the Slave Trade: An Exhibition on the Role of the Gambia in Suppressing the Transatlantic Slavery Trade. Banjul: National Centre for Arts and Culture, 2021.

Parson, Elsie Clews. *Folk Lore of the Sea Islands: South Carolina.* Cambridge, MA: Cosmos Press, 1923.

Rhyne, Nancy. *Before and After Freedom: Lowcountry Folklore and Narratives.* Charleston, SC: The History Press, 2005.

Sona Mariama: Folktales from the Gambia. Banjul: National Centre for Arts and Culture, 2019.

South Carolina Folk Tales: Stories of Animals and Supernatural Beings. Columbia: Federal Writers' Program of South Carolina, 1941.

Talley, Thomas. *The Negro Traditions.* Knoxville: University of Tennessee Press, 1993.

Woodson, Carter G. *African Myths Together with Proverbs.* Washington, D.C.: Associated Publishers, 1928.

Government Documents

Congressional Record, 43rd Congress, 1st Session. Vol. 2, part 1. Washington, D.C.: Government Printing Office, 1874.

Proceedings of the Constitutional Convention of South Carolina Held at Charleston, S.C., Beginning January 14th and Ending March 17th, 1868, Including the Debates and Proceedings. Charleston, SC: Denny and Perry, 1868.

Slave Narratives: South Carolina. Vol. 14. Washington, D.C.: Federal Writers' Project, 1936–38.

Slave Narratives: Texas. Vol. 16. Washington, D.C.: Federal Writers' Project, 1936–38.

Manuscript Collections

Aimar, Leonarda J. "Stories Collected from Slaves." Charleston, SC: College of Charleston, Addlestone Library Archives, Agatha A. Simmons Collection.

Federal Writers' Project: Historical and Education. South Carolina Negro Writers' Project. Manuscripts Division, South Caroliniana Library, University of South Carolina, Columbia, South Carolina. 1936–37.

Federal Writers' Project. "Unpublished Ex-Slave Narratives of South Carolina." Columbia, SC: University of South Carolina, South Caroliniana Library, 1936–37.

Newspapers

Charleston Mercury
Charleston News and Courier
Columbia Palmetto Post
Columbia State
Spartanburg Herald Journal

Scholarly Papers

Graichen, Jody. "Reinterpreting South Carolina History: The South Carolina Negro Writers' Project, 1936–1937." Master's thesis, University of South Carolina, 2005.

Index

About the Author

Damon L. Fordham was born in Spartanburg, South Carolina, and raised in Mount Pleasant, South Carolina, near Charleston. A graduate of the University of South Carolina and the College of Charleston, he is the author of five books, a public lecturer, a tour guide, a storyteller and an adjunct professor of history at The Citadel. He has lectured in America, Canada, West Africa and numerous foreign and domestic media outlets.